Medicare Mastered: A Strategic Guide to Coverage, Costs, and Choices

Jamie L. Kranking

I dedicate this book to my wife, Renee, and son, Mason. Without their love and support, I would never have embraced a personally rewarding career. It is a gift to wake up every day knowing you may be able to help someone.

Medicare Mastered: A Strategic Guide to Coverage, Costs, and Choices

Published by CFH Press, Ponte Vedra Beach, Florida

Disclaimer This book is intended for educational and informational purposes only. It provides general guidance about Medicare rules, options, costs, and enrollment as they exist in 2026. Medicare policies, premiums, deductibles, coverage rules, and benefit structures change annually and can vary based on individual circumstances, location, and eligibility.

The information contained in this book is not a substitute for professional advice. Readers should always verify the most current Medicare rules, costs, and options directly with official sources such as Medicare.gov, 1-800-MEDICARE, or the Social Security Administration. For personalized guidance regarding eligibility, plan selection, coordination with other insurance, or any financial or medical decisions, consult a licensed Medicare broker, qualified insurance advisor, or healthcare professional.

The author and publisher make no representations or warranties of any kind, express or implied, regarding the accuracy, completeness, or suitability of the information in this book. Neither the author nor the publisher shall be liable for any errors, omissions, or damages arising from the use of this material. Decisions about Medicare coverage are the sole responsibility of the reader.

First Edition
ISBN (Paperback): 979-8-9954898-0-1
ISBN (eBook): 979-8-9954898-1-8

Library of Congress Control Number: 2026910784

Printed in the United States of America

Table of Contents

Chapter 1

Introduction to Medicare

Welcome to Medicare Mastered. If you are picking up this book, chances are you are turning 65 soon, helping a parent or spouse navigate their options, or facing Medicare earlier due to a disability. Maybe the mail has started arriving with confusing envelopes from the government, or a friend casually mentioned "Part A this" and "Part B that," and suddenly everything feels a lot more complicated than you expected.

You are not alone, and you are exactly where you need to be.

Medicare is the federal health insurance program that helps millions of Americans cover essential medical care. It was created in 1965 to make sure people 65 and older, as well as some younger individuals with certain qualifying conditions, would not have to choose between groceries and doctor visits. Today, in 2026, Medicare provides peace of mind to over 70 million people, helping cover hospital stays, doctor appointments, preventive screenings, prescription drugs, and much more.

At its core, Medicare is simply health insurance designed for the people who qualify. It works differently from the private insurance you may have
had through an employer, and it is different from Medicaid, the program that helps low-income individuals and families. Medicare was designed for seniors and people with qualifying disabilities, providing reliable coverage backed by the U.S. government.

Medicare is not one-size-fits-all, and that is perfectly okay. It breaks down into four main parts: hospital insurance, medical insurance, prescription drugs, and an all-in-one alternative. Each is designed to work together so you can build protection that fits your life. We will walk through every part clearly and in full detail in the chapters ahead.

Whether you are newly eligible, reviewing your current coverage, or simply planning ahead for peace of mind, the goal of this book is simple: give you the knowledge and confidence to choose coverage that protects your health and your wallet without unnecessary stress.

In the pages ahead, you will find straightforward information, real-world examples, helpful checklists, and practical tips drawn from my years as a Medicare broker helping thousands of people just like you.

As the owner of Care For Healthcare, I am proud to serve clients across the United States, and I am here to simplify the entire process for you. There are no sales pitches here. Just clear answers and honest guidance because you deserve nothing less.

A note about me: I did not come to Medicare professionally. I came to it personally, as a husband, researching every option available when my wife was diagnosed with Stage IV breast cancer. That experience changed everything. It is why I left a career in technology to help others navigate these decisions with clarity and without fear. Every chapter in this book is written with that mission in mind.

The decisions ahead are significant, but you are no longer walking into them alone. Let's get started!

Chapter 2

Who Qualifies for Medicare?

Now that you have a big picture view of what Medicare is and why it exists, the next logical question is this: Do I actually qualify?

The good news is that Medicare eligibility rules are straightforward for most people. The program is designed to cover seniors and certain individuals with disabilities or specific serious conditions. In 2026, the core requirements remain consistent with recent years, but it is always smart to confirm your personal situation with official sources or a trusted advisor. Once you understand these simple rules, a lot of uncertainty disappears.

Let us break it down step by step with clear examples and a checklist you can use right now.

The Main Path: Turning 65

Most people become eligible for Medicare when they reach age 65. This is the classic entry point, and it is automatic for many.

You must be a U.S. citizen or a lawful permanent resident (green card holder) who has lived in the United States continuously for at least five years. Your eligibility starts the month you turn 65 (or the month before, if your birthday falls on the first of the month).

If you are already receiving Social Security retirement benefits or Railroad Retirement Board benefits, you will usually be enrolled automatically in both Part A and Part B starting on the first day of the month you become eligible. That is one less thing to keep track of.

If you are not yet receiving those benefits, perhaps you are still working or choosing to delay Social Security. You will need to sign up manually during your Initial Enrollment Period. Enrollment is covered in detail in Chapter 11.

Real Life Example

Maria turns 65 on July 15, 2026. Her Medicare Initial Enrollment Period can start as early as April 1 (three months before her birth month). If she signs up in time, her coverage can begin July 1. But if she waits until her actual birthday month, coverage typically starts August 1. If she is already receiving Social Security, everything kicks in automatically on July 1. No extra steps needed. Simple moments like this show how the system is built to make the transition as easy as possible.

Qualifying Earlier: Disability or Specific Conditions

You do not have to wait until age 65 if you have a qualifying disability or certain medical conditions. Medicare steps in to help when serious health issues arise, no matter what your age. You can qualify as soon as you meet the program's definition of disability, provided you have sufficient work credits.

If you are under 65 and receiving Social Security Disability Insurance (SSDI) benefits (or certain Railroad Retirement Board disability benefits), Medicare eligibility begins after you have received those benefits for 24 full months. Coverage starts on the 25th month. This built-in waiting period allows other coverage, such as employer plans, to take effect first.

For ALS (Amyotrophic Lateral Sclerosis, also known as Lou Gehrig's disease), there is no 24-month wait. If you qualify for SSDI because of ALS, Medicare starts the same month your disability benefits begin, sometimes immediately upon approval.

For End-Stage Renal Disease (ESRD), which is permanent kidney failure that requires regular dialysis or a kidney transplant, you can qualify for Medicare at any age. Coverage often starts the first month of dialysis (or after a short waiting period in some cases). You or a family member must also meet the basic work-history rules.

These exceptional cases make sure Medicare is there for people facing major health challenges, regardless of age. The rules exist to provide support exactly when it's needed most.

Premium-Free Part A: The Role of Work History

Here is where your (or your spouse's) work record comes in, and it is one of the most frequent questions I receive from clients. If you do not have enough work credits on your own record, you may qualify through a spouse's work history (living, deceased, or divorced).

Part A (hospital insurance) is premium-free for most people because they (or their spouse) paid Medicare taxes through payroll deductions during their working years. To qualify for premium-free Part A in 2026, you (or your spouse living or deceased) generally need at least 40 quarters of coverage, often called credits. This amounts to roughly 10 years of work during which Social Security and Medicare taxes were paid. You can earn up to 4 credits per year (in 2026, roughly $1,810 in earnings per credit; the exact amount is adjusted annually; check www.ssa.gov for your record).

Certain federal, state, or local government employees hired before specific dates may also qualify through their own work history.

If you do not have enough credits, you can still buy Part A. With 30 to 39 quarters, the monthly premium is $311 in 2026. With fewer than 30 quarters, the full premium is $565 per month in 2026.

Part B (medical insurance) always has a monthly premium (the standard amount is around $202.90 in 2026 for most people, but greater for higher incomes due to the IRMAA surcharge. We go into more details about IRMAA in Chapter 10. Note: You can enroll in Part B even if you pay for Part A.

Eligibility Checklist

• Turning 65 or older? Yes, means you're eligible (citizenship and residency rules apply).
 • Under 65 and receiving SSDI for 24 months or more? Yes, means you are eligible.
• Diagnosed with ALS and approved for disability benefits? Yes, means immediate eligibility.
• Have ESRD requiring dialysis or a transplant? Yes, means you're likely eligible (check work history).
• 40 or more quarters of work credits (you or your spouse)? Yes, means premium-free Part A.
• U.S. citizen or lawful permanent resident for five continuous years or more? Yes, means you meet the basic requirement.

If any part feels unclear, pull your Social Security statement at www.ssa.gov/myaccount or call 1-800-772-1213. It's free and quick.

Myths vs. Facts

- **Myth:** You must be retired to get Medicare.
    - **Fact:** You can be working full-time and still qualify at 65. Many people keep their employer coverage and delay Part B (coordination is covered in Chapter 13).
- **Myth:** Medicare is only for low-income people.
    - **Fact:** It is for qualifying seniors and disabled individuals, regardless of income (though help is available for lower incomes through programs like Extra Help or Medicare Savings Programs; see Chapter 10).
- **Myth: Medicare covers everything, so you don't need additional insurance.**
    - **Fact:** Original Medicare has no out-of-pocket maximum, meaning your costs can be unlimited if you have a serious illness or extended hospital stay. There are deductibles, copays, and significant gaps, including the lack of dental, vision, or hearing coverage. That's exactly why Medigap and Medicare Advantage plans exist.

- **Myth: Once you choose a Medicare plan, you're locked in forever.**
  - **Fact:** You have opportunities every year to review and change your coverage. The Annual Enrollment Period (October 15 to December 7) allows you to switch plans, drop coverage, or add Part D. You are never permanently locked into a decision you made at 65 (see Chapter 18).

What If I Don't Qualify?

If you do not meet these criteria? For example, if you haven't lived in the U.S. long enough as a permanent resident, or you don't have a qualifying disability, you will not be eligible for Medicare. Alternatives include Marketplace plans (healthcare.gov), Medicaid (if you have low income), or private insurance. Most readers of this book will qualify through age or disability, however.

Understanding eligibility removes a big layer of worry. Once you know you qualify, the next steps are learning exactly what each part of Medicare covers (starting in Chapter 3) and when and how to enroll without penalties.

Knowing you qualify is the first step. Now it's time to understand exactly what you're qualifying for.

Chapter 3

The Four Parts of Medicare

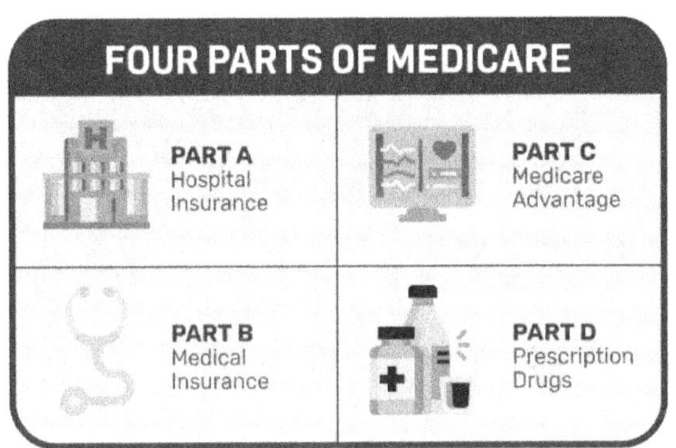

Welcome to one of the most important chapters in
**Medicare Mastered: A Strategic Guide to Coverage,
Costs, and Choices**. If Medicare feels like an alphabet
soup at first, you are not alone! The program breaks
down into four main "parts" labeled A, B, C, and D, each
covering distinct aspects of healthcare.

Think of them as simple building blocks: Parts A and B
form the solid foundation (known together as Original
Medicare). In contrast, Parts C and D offer flexible ways
to customize or expand your coverage through private
insurance companies. Each part will be explored in much
more detail later in the book, but here is a clear,

straightforward overview to help you see the full picture and feel more in control right from the start.

Part A: Hospital Insurance

Part A focuses on inpatient and facility-based care. It helps pay for the times when you need to be admitted to a hospital or receive structured support in a skilled nursing facility or hospice.

What Part A Covers in 2026:

- Inpatient hospital stays (semi-private room, meals, nursing care, and necessary supplies during your stay).
- Skilled nursing facility care (after a qualifying 3-day hospital stay, mainly for rehabilitation or recovery).
- Hospice care (for terminal illnesses, including pain relief, symptom management, and emotional support services).
- Some home health care (part-time skilled nursing, physical therapy, or other services if you are homebound and meet the criteria).

Most people get Part A premium-free if they or their spouse worked and paid Medicare taxes for at least 10 years (40 quarters). If not, you can still buy it (premiums range from $311 to $565 per month in 2026, depending on your work credits).

Costs You Might Incur:

- **Monthly Premium**
- **Inpatient Hospital Deductible**
- **Hospital Copays**
- **Hospital Coinsurance**
- **Skilled Nursing Copays**
- **Hospice Copays and Coinsurance**
- **No Maximum Out-of-Pocket**

Part B: Medical Insurance

Part B covers outpatient and preventive care. It is the part most people think of when they picture routine doctor visits and staying healthy day to day.

What Part B Covers in 2026:

- Doctor visits and services from other providers (nurse practitioners, therapists, etc.).
- Emergency room visits.
- Outpatient care (surgeries, tests, X-rays, and lab work done without being admitted to the hospital).
- Preventive services (annual wellness visits, many screenings, vaccines like flu and pneumonia, and more—often at no cost if your provider accepts Medicare assignment).

- Durable medical equipment (wheelchairs, walkers, oxygen, hospital beds for home use).
- Home health care (if skilled care is needed and you are homebound).
- Limited outpatient prescription drugs (such as injections given in a doctor's office or chemotherapy drugs).

Part B always has a monthly premium. You must enroll to get Part B, and most people pay this premium. If your income exceeds certain levels due to IRMAA surcharges, your premium will be higher. IRMAA is explained in detail in Chapter 10.

Costs You Might Incur:

- **Monthly Premium**
- **Annual Deductible**
- **Copays**
- **Coinsurance**
- **Late Enrollment Penalty**
- **IRMAA**
- **No Maximum Out-of-Pocket**

Part C: Medicare Advantage

Part C, also called Medicare Advantage, is an all-in-one alternative to Original Medicare. Private insurance companies offer these plans, which Medicare approves. They must cover at least everything that Original Medicare (Parts A and B) covers (except hospice in some cases), and most plans include Part D prescription drug coverage.

What Part C Covers:

- Extra benefits not included in Original Medicare, such as vision exams and glasses, dental cleanings, hearing aids, fitness programs like SilverSneakers®, over-the-counter allowances, transportation to medical appointments, meal delivery after hospital stays, and more. These extras vary by plan and can make a significant difference in daily life.
- Usually prescription drugs (conveniently bundled in).

Many plans have a $0 additional premium on top of your Part B premium, though some charge a small additional premium. They often use provider networks (you stay in-network for the lowest costs) and include an annual out-of-pocket maximum (a yearly cap often $5,000–$10,000 depending on the plan, after which you pay nothing more for covered services the rest of the year).

Pros: Convenience, extra benefits, and potentially lower out-of-pocket costs for many people.

Cons: Networks and prior approvals for some services, which means less flexibility than Original Medicare.

Part D: Prescription Drug Coverage

Part D helps pay for the medications you take at home.

What Part D covers:

- Brand-name and generic prescription drugs.
- Most vaccines and shots (such as the shingles vaccine) are recommended by your doctor.
- Insulin (capped at $35 per month supply in many cases).

You can get Part D through a standalone plan added to Original Medicare or bundled into most Medicare Advantage plans. Because private companies run these plans, the list of covered drugs (formulary), costs, and participating pharmacies can vary from plan to plan.

Costs You Might Incur:

- **Monthly Premium**
- **Deductible**
- **Copays/Coinsurance**
- **Annual Out-of-Pocket Maximum**
- **Late Enrollment Penalty**
- **IRMAA**

Quick Reference: The Four Parts at a Glance (2026)

PART	WHAT IT COVERS	KEY COSTS (2026)	NOTES
Part A	Inpatient hospital, skilled nursing, hospice, and some home health	Premium: Usually $0; Deductible $1,736 per benefit period; Copays; 20% Coinsurance	Premium-free for most with 10+ years work history
Part B	Doctor visits, outpatient care, preventive services, durable equipment	Premium $202.90/month standard; Deductible $283/year; Copays; 20% Coinsurance	Always has premium; preventive services often $0; avoid late penalty
Part C (Medicare Advantage)	All of A & B, usually D, plus extras (vision, dental, hearing, etc.)	Varies; Many $0 extra premium; Yearly out-of-pocket max	Private plans; networks common
Part D	Prescription drugs from pharmacy	Premium varies (~$34.50 avg standalone); Deductible up to $615; $2,100 out-of-pocket cap	Standalone or bundled; avoid late penalty

The next chapters offer a much deeper dive into each part, starting with Part A. In Chapter 10, there is a deep dive into 2026 costs.

Understanding these four parts helps people avoid surprises and make choices that truly fit their needs. If questions come up as you read, jot them down, as they will be addressed in the chapters ahead. The foundation is set. Every chapter ahead builds on what you just learned.

Chapter 4

Part A - Hospital Insurance

When most people think of Medicare, they picture coverage for hospital stays, and that's exactly what Medicare Part A provides. Officially called Hospital Insurance, Part A forms the foundation of Original Medicare. It helps pay for inpatient care when you're seriously ill or injured, plus a few other important facility-based services.

The good news? Most people receive Part A completely premium-free because they (or their spouse) paid Medicare taxes through work for at least 10 years. It is important to clearly understand what Part A covers and, just as importantly, what it doesn't. This knowledge gives you the confidence to plan ahead and avoid unexpected costs.

In this chapter, we'll walk through exactly what Part A includes, how the costs work in 2026 (with the latest deductibles, copays, and coinsurance), the simple idea of "benefit periods," real-life examples, handy checklists, and practical tips to help you make the most of your coverage.

What Does Medicare Part A Cover?

Part A focuses on inpatient and facility-based care. Here's a clear breakdown of the main benefits it provides:

- **Inpatient hospital care**: This includes a semi-private room, meals, general nursing, inpatient prescription drugs given as part of your hospital treatment, and other medically necessary services. Part A covers care in acute care hospitals, critical access hospitals, inpatient rehabilitation facilities, and inpatient psychiatric facilities. (Private rooms, TVs, phones, or personal comfort items are usually not covered unless medically necessary.)
- **Skilled nursing facility (SNF) care**: If you need daily skilled care after a qualifying 3-day inpatient hospital stay (such as physical therapy or IV medications), Part A covers up to 100 days per

benefit period in a Medicare-certified skilled nursing facility.

- **Hospice care:** For terminally ill patients with a life expectancy of 6 months or less who choose comfort care instead of curative treatment. Part A covers most hospice services, including pain relief, emotional and spiritual support, and many drugs for symptom management.
- **Home health care:** Limited skilled nursing, physical therapy, speech therapy, or occupational therapy in your own home if you are homebound and meet the criteria.
- **Blood:** The first 3 pints of blood per benefit period are not covered; you are responsible for those.

Part A does **not** cover long-term custodial care (help with everyday activities like bathing or dressing), most outpatient services (those fall under Part B), or private-duty nursing.

How Costs Work in 2026

Costs depend on the type of service and how long you need care. The great news for most people is that the monthly premium for Part A is $0 (premium-free if you or your spouse paid Medicare taxes for 10 or more years).

If you don't have enough work credits, you can still buy Part A; however, the 2026 monthly premium ranges from $311 (for 30–39 quarters) to $565.

Here are the key 2026 out-of-pocket costs (these amounts are updated each year by Medicare):

- **Inpatient Hospital Deductible:** $1,736 per benefit period. Think of this as a "reset" fee you pay each time you start a new benefit period after being out of any hospital or skilled nursing facility for 60 consecutive days.
- **Hospital Copays:**
    - Days 1–60: $0 after the deductible.
    - Days 61–90: $434 per day.
    - Days 91–150: $868 per day. Once you exhaust your lifetime reserve days, you pay 100% of all costs. (You only get 60 reserve days in your lifetime, so use them carefully.
- **Coinsurance**: 20% of the amount approved by Medicare for services after your deductible
- **Skilled Nursing Facility Coinsurance:**
    - Days 1–20: $0 (after a qualifying 3-day hospital stay).
    - Days 21–100: $217 per day.
    - After day 100: You pay 100% of all costs.

- **Other Notes:** Hospice and home health care usually have $0 cost for covered services, though small copays and coinsurance may apply for some hospice drugs or respite care.

IMPORTANT REMINDER: Original Medicare Part A has **no annual out-of-pocket maximum**. This means costs can add up during a long hospital stay or multiple stays in a year. That's exactly why so many people add a Medigap plan or choose a Medicare Advantage plan. They provide extra protection and peace of mind.

Understanding Benefit Periods

A "benefit period" is how Medicare counts your hospital or skilled nursing facility coverage. It is not based on the calendar year. The benefit period begins the day you are admitted as an inpatient and ends only after you have been out of any hospital or skilled nursing facility for 60 consecutive days.

This means you can have more than one benefit period in the same year, and you may need to pay the $1,736 deductible again for each new period.

Real Life Examples

> *1.   You are hospitalized in March for surgery, go home and recover for 70 days, then need hospital care again in October. Because more than 60 days have passed, this starts a brand-new benefit period, and you pay the deductible again and the copay count starts over.*
>
> *2.   A single 75-day hospital stay would cost you the $1,736 deductible plus $434 per day for days 61–75 (15 days), totaling more than $8,246 in out-of-pocket costs before any extra coverage, plus 20% coinsurance on services. These examples show why planning ahead with additional coverage can protect your savings.*

Common Questions and Helpful Tips

- **Do I need to enroll?** If you are already receiving Social Security, Part A usually starts automatically when you turn 65. If not, be sure to sign up during your Initial Enrollment Period to avoid penalties.
- **What if I still have employer coverage?** Part A can work together with group health plans. Properly coordinating the two can save you money.
- **Is Part A coverage truly comprehensive?** Not entirely. Part A has no yearly out-of-pocket maximum or lifetime limit on hospital days, meaning a long hospital stay can lead to high costs.

This is where a Medigap policy or a well-chosen Medicare Advantage plan can provide valuable extra protection.

Checklist: Making the Most of Part A

- Confirm your work credits at www.ssa.gov.
- Keep good records of all hospitals and skilled nursing facility stays.
- Talk with your doctor early about home health or hospice options when they may be appropriate.
- Consider adding a Medigap or a Medicare Advantage plan for stronger protection against large hospital bills.

Part A gives you essential protection during major health events. Taking a few minutes to understand the details now can save you stress and money later.

In the next chapter, we will dive into Medicare Part B (Medical Insurance) and explore how it covers doctor visits, outpatient care, preventive services, and more. Part A is the floor of your Medicare house. Now let's build the walls.

Chapter 5

Part B - Medical Insurance

If Medicare Part A is your safety net for hospital stays, Medicare Part B is the coverage that helps with the everyday medical needs you're likely to use as you age. Officially called Medical Insurance, Part B pays a sizable portion of costs for doctor visits, preventive services, outpatient care, and much more.

Most people pay a monthly premium for Part B, and unlike Part A, it is never premium-free. Still, it is an essential piece for well-rounded protection. It is critical to understand the details of Part B, such as the costs, and the ability to pair it with the right supplement or plan to keep surprises to a minimum.

In this chapter, we'll cover exactly what Part B includes, the 2026 costs (including the latest premium and deductible), how copays and coinsurance work, the valuable preventive benefits, real-life examples, and practical tips to help you get the most value from your coverage.

What Does Medicare Part B Cover?

Part B focuses on outpatient and non-hospital care. It is the kind of healthcare service most people need regularly. Here is a clear breakdown of the key services it provides:

- **Doctor and provider services:** Office visits, consultations, approved second opinions, and care from specialists, as long as the provider accepts Medicare assignment.
- **Outpatient care:** Services received in hospital outpatient departments, clinics, or ambulatory surgical centers (for example, same-day surgeries, X-rays, MRIs, or lab work).
- **Preventive services:** Many are available at $0 cost, including annual wellness visits, flu shots, pneumonia vaccines, diabetes screenings, mammogram screenings, colonoscopies, cardiovascular screenings, and depression screenings.
- **Durable medical equipment (DME):** Items such as as wheelchairs, walkers, oxygen equipment, hospital

beds, or CPAP machines when prescribed for home use.

- **Home health care:** Skilled nursing, physical therapy, speech therapy, or occupational therapy in your home if you are homebound and a doctor orders it (no 3-day hospital stay required).
- **Outpatient mental health services:** Therapy, counseling, and partial hospitalization programs.
- **Ambulance services:** When medically necessary (for example, transport to a hospital or dialysis facility).
- **Certain outpatient prescription drugs:** Drugs administered by a provider, such as chemotherapy, injections, or infusions (self-administered drugs you pick up at the pharmacy fall under Part D instead).

Part B does **not** cover routine dental, vision, or hearing exams and hearing aids (except in a few limited situations), most prescription drugs you take at home (that's Part D), long-term custodial care, cosmetic procedures, or acupuncture (with only a few exceptions).

How Costs Work in 2026

Part B has fairly predictable costs, and like Part A, has no annual out-of-pocket maximum. This means the 20% coinsurance can add up significantly for frequent doctor visits or expensive outpatient treatments, which is why many people add a Medigap plan or choose a Medicare Advantage plan for better protection.

Key 2026 Costs:

- **Monthly Premium:** The standard amount is $202.90 per month for most people. This is usually deducted automatically from your Social Security check. If you don't receive Social Security, you will be billed quarterly in advance.
- **Annual Deductible:** $283 for the year. You pay this once per calendar year before Part B begins sharing costs.
- **Preventive Services & Some Clinical Lab Tests:** Often $0 (no deductible or coinsurance for many covered preventive services).
- **Copays:** A fixed dollar amount you pay for a specific service or item. For example, you may pay $20 for a doctor's visit.

- **Coinsurance:** After you meet the deductible, you typically pay 20% of the Medicare-approved amount for most services, while Medicare pays the remaining 80% as long as your provider accepts Medicare assignment.

- **Income-Related Monthly Adjustment Amount (IRMAA):** If your modified adjusted gross income from two years earlier exceeds certain thresholds (starting at about $109,000 for an individual or $218,000 for a joint return), you will pay a higher monthly premium, which is up to $689.90 or more in 2026. Social Security will notify you if this applies to you.

Key Preventive Benefits at $0 Cost

One of the best features of Part B is the wide range of preventive services that are often completely free. These services are designed to help catch health issues early, when they are usually easier and less expensive to treat.

- Annual wellness visit (which creates a personalized prevention plan).
- Cancer screenings (breast, cervical, colorectal), diabetes screenings, cardiovascular screenings.
- Vaccines (flu, pneumococcal, hepatitis B, and COVID-19 when covered).

- Bone density tests, glaucoma screenings, and many others.

Helpful Tip: Always ask your provider to code the visit as "preventive" so you receive the $0 benefit. A quick confirmation can save you from unexpected bills.

Real Life Examples

> *1.   Sarah schedules her annual wellness visit and a mammogram screening. Because both services are coded as preventative, she pays nothing. Later in the year, she sees her doctor for a routine checkup, meets her deductible, and then pays copays and 20% coinsurance on the approved amount.*
>
> *2.   A single outpatient MRI can cost the deductible plus 20% of the Medicare-approved amount, which is often several hundred dollars.*

These everyday examples show why many people add extra coverage to protect against the accumulation of coinsurance costs.

Common Questions and Tips

- **Enrollment:** Most people enroll in Part B during their Initial Enrollment Period around age 65. If you delay without having creditable coverage (such as employer group health), you may face a permanent

10% lifetime premium penalty for each year you delay.

- **Provider choice:** Stick with doctors and providers who accept Medicare assignments to avoid excess charges (up to 15% more than the approved amount).
- **Gaps to watch:** Because Original Medicare has no annual out-of-pocket maximum, the 20% coinsurance can add up quickly, especially with frequent care or a catastrophic illness. A Medigap plan can cover some or all of that 20%, while many Medicare Advantage plans include a yearly cap for greater peace of mind.

Checklist: Getting the Most from Part B

- Schedule your preventive services every year.
- Choose providers who accept Medicare assignment.
- Review your IRMAA situation if your income has changed.
- Consider pairing Part B with a Medicare Supplement (Medigap) or a Medicare Advantage plan for stronger financial protection.

Part B keeps you covered for routine and preventive care and works hand-in-hand with Part A to give you solid Original Medicare protection. Taking time to understand these details now helps you budget wisely and protect your savings for years to come.

Part A and Part B each cover their own domain, and together, they are the foundation on which everything else is built.

Part B - Medical Insurance

Chapter 6

Part C - Medicare Advantage

By now, you've seen the solid foundation that Original Medicare provides and how Medicare Supplement Plans (Medigap) can fill its gaps. But there is another popular path many people choose: Medicare Advantage, also known as Part C.

Private insurance companies approved by Medicare offer Medicare Advantage plans. Instead of getting your hospital and medical coverage directly from the government and adding supplements or separate drug plans, you enroll in one private plan that bundles everything together.

These plans must cover at least what Original Medicare covers, and most go well beyond that by including prescription drug coverage and valuable extra benefits.

Many people are drawn to Medicare Advantage for its lower monthly costs, built-in out-of-pocket limits, and added perks like dental, vision, and hearing coverage.

In this chapter, we'll explore how Medicare Advantage works in 2026, the common types of plans, costs, benefits, potential drawbacks, and practical tips to help you decide if it's the right fit for your needs.

How Medicare Advantage Works

When you join a Medicare Advantage plan, the private insurer takes the place of Original Medicare for your day-to-day health coverage (except hospice care, which remains under Part A). You still pay your monthly Part B premium (plus any income-related adjustment, and the plan may charge its own additional premium, often $0 or very low.

Most Medicare Advantage plans include:
- All Part A hospital and Part B medical services that Original Medicare covers.
- Prescription drug plan.
- An annual out-of-pocket maximum that protects you from very high costs (many plans cap in-network

spending at $9,250 or less in 2026; some set even lower limits between $4,000 and $7,000).
- Extra benefits not found in Original Medicare, such as routine dental cleanings, vision exams and glasses, hearing aids, fitness programs like SilverSneakers®, over-the-counter allowances, and transportation to medical appointments.

You usually receive care from providers within the plan's network, and some plans require referrals for specialists or prior authorization for certain services. Emergency care is always covered anywhere in the United States, and urgent care is typically covered as well.

Common Types of Medicare Advantage Plans

Plans come in different structures, so you can choose the level of flexibility that matches your lifestyle:
- **HMO (Health Maintenance Organization):** Usually lower premiums and copays, but you generally must stay in-network (except for emergencies) and often need referrals for specialists.
- **PPO (Preferred Provider Organization):** More flexibility to see out-of-network providers (at higher cost) and usually no referrals required for specialists.
- **Special Needs Plans (SNP):** Designed for specific groups, such as people with chronic conditions (like diabetes or heart disease), those who qualify for both Medicare and Medicaid, or individuals living in nursing homes.

- **Private Fee-for-Service (PFFS):** Less common and not available everywhere; these let you see any Medicare-accepting provider, but the plan sets its own payment terms.

In most areas, you will have many options, including numerous $0-premium plans.

Medicare Advantage Costs in 2026

Costs vary by plan, your location, and your specific health needs:

- **Monthly Premium:** Average around $14 in addition to your Part B premium for plans that include drug coverage; many popular plans have a $0 additional premium.
- **Deductibles, Copays, and Coinsurance:** These are usually fixed amounts instead of the 20% coinsurance in Original Medicare (for example, $0–$50 for doctor visits or set copays for hospital stays).
- **Out-of-Pocket Maximum:** This is one of the biggest advantages. Once you reach the yearly cap on covered services (often $4,000–$9,250 in-network), the plan pays 100% of additional covered costs for the rest of the year.
- **Prescription Drugs:** Monthly premium for prescription coverage is included in most plans, with the same $2,100 out-of-pocket cap that applies to standalone Part D.

Benefits and Potential Drawbacks

Advantages many clients appreciate:

- Predictable costs thanks to the yearly out-of-pocket maximum, which protects against high bills from serious or prolonged illness.
- Extra benefits like routine dental, vision, hearing aids, fitness programs, and transportation may be included in the plan.
- Often $0 or incredibly low additional monthly premiums.
- Built-in care coordination can be especially helpful since everything is under one plan.

Potential drawbacks to consider:

- Provider networks may limit your choice of doctors and hospitals (always check that your current providers are in-network).
- Some plans require prior authorization or referrals, which can add steps before certain care.
- If you later want to switch back to Original Medicare and buy a Medigap policy, you may face health questions and possible denial or higher rates.
- Benefits and networks can change each year, so it's important to review your plan during Medicare Advantage Open Enrollment (January 1st through March 31st) or the Annual Election Period (October 15 to December 7).

For healthy individuals who rarely need care, a low-premium Medicare Advantage plan with extras can be a smart money-saver. For people who see specialists frequently, travel often, or want maximum provider choice, Original Medicare plus a Medigap supplement often feels more comfortable.

Choosing a Medicare Advantage Plan

The best way to find the right plan is to compare options carefully. You can use Medicare.gov/plan-compare or work with an independent Medicare broker who can review plans based on your doctors, medications, and budget.

Helpful tips:
- Make sure your regular doctors, specialists, and pharmacies are in the plan's network.
- Check that your current prescriptions are on the plan's formulary and review the copay tiers.
- Look at the plan's star ratings (1 to 5 stars) for overall quality and member satisfaction.
- Compare out-of-pocket maximums, copays, and the extra benefits that matter most to you.
- Enroll during your Initial Enrollment Period or the Annual Election Period (October 15 to December 7) to avoid restrictions.

Medicare Advantage has grown in popularity because it simplifies coverage and adds real value for many people. In the next chapter, we will take a closer look at prescription drug coverage (Part D), so you understand how it works, whether you choose Original Medicare or a Medicare Advantage plan.

Medicare Advantage isn't right for everyone, but for the right person, it can be the smartest move they make at 65. Now you know how to tell the difference.

Chapter 7

Part D - Prescription Drug Coverage

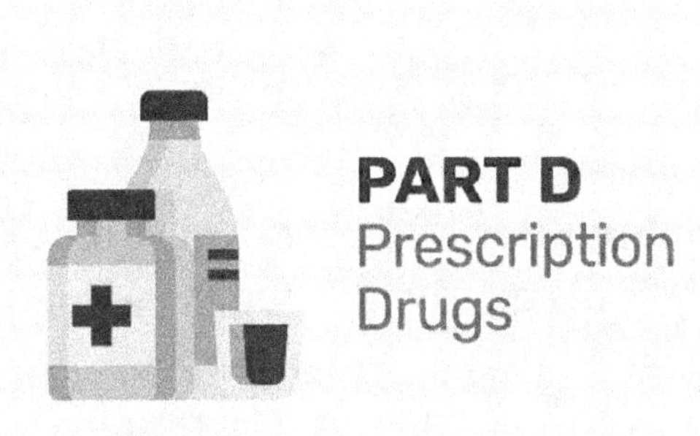

Prescription medications play a significant role in staying healthy as we age, whether for managing chronic conditions like diabetes, high blood pressure, or heart disease, or for short-term needs after an illness or surgery. Medicare helps cover these costs through prescription drug coverage, which comes in two main forms: standalone Medicare Part D plans (often paired with Original Medicare) or built into Medicare Advantage plans (called MA-PD plans).

It is critical to review your current prescriptions, compare plans side by side, and find a plan that minimizes your expenses while ensuring your important drugs are included. In this chapter, we will explore how Part D and Medicare Advantage drug coverage work in 2026, the key costs and critical changes, practical ways to manage your medications, and tips to avoid common pitfalls.

How Prescription Drug Coverage Works

You can get prescription drug coverage in one of two ways:

- **Standalone Part D Prescription Drug Plan (PDP):** This pairs with Original Medicare (Parts A and B) and often a Medigap policy. It covers self-administered outpatient prescriptions such as pills, inhalers, creams, and injectables you take at home.
- **Medicare Advantage Plan with Drug Coverage (MA-PD):** This bundles Parts A, B, and usually Part D into one convenient plan, along with extras like dental or vision.

Both options use a **formulary**, which is a list of covered drugs organized into tiers (generics are usually the lowest-cost; brand-name drugs are higher-cost). Some plans may require step therapy, prior authorization, or quantity limits for certain medications. That's why it's always important to check the formulary for your specific drugs before you enroll.

Thanks to the Inflation Reduction Act, 2026 brings more predictability and protection. There is no more "donut hole," a clear annual out-of-pocket cap, and the new

Medicare Prescription Payment Plan that lets you spread costs over the year if you prefer.

Key Features and Costs in 2026

Costs vary by plan, your location, and your medications, but here are the important 2026 benchmarks:

- **Annual Out-of-Pocket Cap:** $2,100 for covered Part D drugs. This includes what you spend on deductibles, copays, and coinsurance. Once you reach $2,100 in a year, you pay $0 for all covered prescriptions for the rest of the year.
- **Deductible:** Up to $615 (many plans have a lower deductible or $0). You pay the full price for drugs until the deductible is met.
- **Copays and Coinsurance:** After the deductible (if any), you typically pay around 25% coinsurance or fixed copays until you reach the $2,100 cap. Many plans offer low fixed copays for generics, often $0–$10.
- **Monthly Premiums:** Average premiums for standalone Part D plans are around $34.50. For Medicare Advantage plans with drug coverage, there is typically no additional premium. Keep in mind, Medicare Advantage premiums are on top of your Part B premium.
- **Insulin:** Capped at $35 per month supply for covered insulin products (no deductible applies).
- **Vaccines:** Most recommended vaccines (shingles, flu, etc.) are covered at $0.
- **Income-Related Monthly Adjustment Amount (IRMAA):** Higher-income beneficiaries may pay a

surcharge that is added to their premiums. (See Chapter 10 for IRMAA details.

Managing Your Medications Effectively

To get the best coverage and the lowest possible costs, follow these practical steps:

- Make a complete list of your current prescriptions, including names, dosages, and the pharmacies you use.
- Compare plans and see which ones cover your drugs at the lowest cost. The formulary search is the most important part.
- Choose preferred pharmacies in the plan's network for the lowest copays.
- Ask your doctor about lower-cost generics, biosimilars, or mail-order options when appropriate.
- If eligible, consider enrolling in the Medicare Prescription Payment Plan if you want to spread your prescription costs evenly throughout the year.
- Check whether you qualify for Extra Help (the Low-Income Subsidy). If you do, it can dramatically reduce or eliminate your premiums and costs.
- Review your coverage every year during the Annual Election Period (October 15 to December 7), because formularies and costs can change.

Common Mistakes to Avoid

- Delaying enrollment in Part D without having creditable drug coverage (this can lead to a permanent late-enrollment penalty).
- Assuming every plan covers the same drugs. Always verify your specific medications on the formulary.
- Overlooking the $2,100 cap, as it provides excellent protection for anyone taking high-cost or multiple medications.

Standalone Part D vs. Medicare Advantage Drug Coverage

A standalone Part D plan gives you maximum flexibility when you stay with Original Medicare and a Medigap supplement. However, you handle drug costs separately (though covered drugs are still capped at $2,100 per year). Medicare Advantage plans bundle drug coverage into a single plan, which can sometimes mean lower copays for your prescriptions and the convenience of everything in one plan.

The right choice depends on your specific medications, your budget, and how much you value flexibility versus extras. Many clients who take multiple or expensive drugs benefit greatly from the $2,100 cap, no matter which route they choose.

In the next chapter, we will cover the key costs of Medicare, including premiums, deductibles, coinsurance, copays, and practical savings tips.

Knowledge is Power! Understanding your prescription drug options is one of the most important steps toward protecting both your health and your budget.

Chapter 8

Filling the Gap

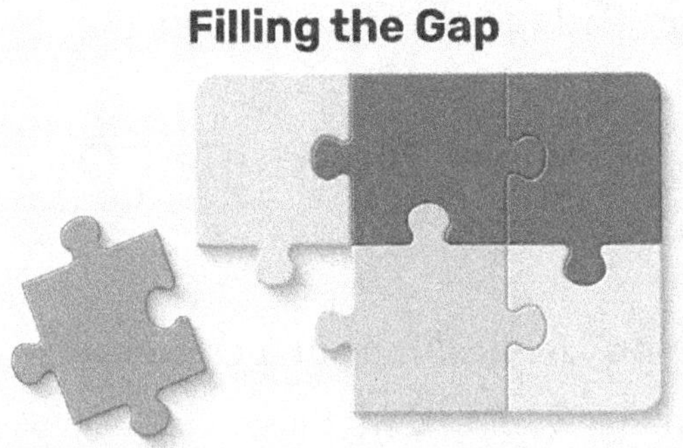

Why Original Medicare Alone Isn't Enough

Now that you've seen how Medicare Parts A and B provide a solid foundation: hospital stays, doctor visits, preventive care, and more. It's reliable government-backed insurance that millions of Americans count on every year.

But here's an important truth I share with clients every single day: Original Medicare (Parts A and B together) still has significant coverage gaps. Those gaps can lead to unexpected, and sometimes extremely high, costs when health challenges arise.

In this chapter, we'll look honestly at the main gaps in Original Medicare, share real-world examples of how costs can add up, and explain why so many people choose to add protection through Medicare Supplement Plans (Medigap) or Medicare Advantage plans.

The Biggest Gap: No Annual Out-of-Pocket Maximum

Unlike most private health insurance and even Medicare Advantage plans, Original Medicare has no yearly cap on what you pay for covered services. You continue paying deductibles, copays, and coinsurance for as long as care continues in that year.

Here are the key 2026 costs that can add up quickly without additional protection:

- **Part A (Hospital Insurance):** $1,736 deductible per benefit period (this period resets after 60 consecutive days out of any hospital or skilled nursing facility). Then, copays apply: you pay $0 for days 1–60, $434 per day for days 61–90, and $868 per day for lifetime reserve days (you get only 60 of these over your entire lifetime). After those lifetime reserve days are used, you pay 100% of the costs. In addition, you must pay your 20% coinsurance for Medicare-approved services provided. Keep in mind that there is no cap on these costs.

- **Part B (Medical Insurance):** $283 annual deductible, copays followed by 20% coinsurance on most services (doctor visits, outpatient surgery, durable medical equipment, etc.). Similar to Part A, there is no cap for Part B. That 20% coinsurance can quickly add up to thousands of dollars for things like chemotherapy, repeated outpatient procedures, or frequent specialist care.

Real Life Example

Imagine an 80-day hospital stay. You could face the $1,736 deductible, $434 per day for 20 days, and 20% coinsurance for approved services. That's already over $10,000 for Part A alone. Add in Part B services such as doctor fees or rehabilitation, and the costs grow fast. Without extra protection, there is no built-in safety net if health issues become serious or long-lasting. Many families are surprised by how quickly these costs can affect their savings.

Other Common Gaps in Original Medicare

In addition to the lack of an out-of-pocket maximum, Original Medicare leaves several other critical areas uncovered or only partially covered:

- **Routine dental, vision, and hearing care:** Cleanings, glasses, contacts, and hearing aids are generally not included (although a few preventive eye or ear screenings may be covered).
- **Skilled nursing facility days:** Limited to 100 days per benefit period, with coinsurance after day 20, and only after a qualifying 3-day hospital stay.
- **Long-term custodial care:** Help with everyday activities, such as bathing, dressing, or eating, is not covered. Medicare pays only for skilled medical care.
- **Prescription drugs:** Part B covers only drugs given by a provider (such as chemotherapy infusions). Self-administered medications you take at home require separate Part D coverage, which has its own $2,100 out-of-pocket cap in 2026.
- **Provider flexibility and extra charges:** If a doctor does not "accept assignment" of Medicare, you may face up to 15% in excess charges on top of your 20% coinsurance.

These gaps are exactly why so many people experience financial stress during an illness, even with what they thought was "good" Medicare coverage. The good news is that you have straightforward ways to close most of these gaps.

How Most People Fill These Gaps

The great news is that you have two excellent, well-tested ways to close most or all of these gaps and protect your savings:

- **Medicare Supplement Plans (also called Medigap):** These are private insurance policies you buy to work alongside Original Medicare (Parts A & B). They help pay deductibles, coinsurance, and copays. Popular options like Plan G often leave you with very predictable, low out-of-pocket costs, sometimes just the Part B deductible of $283 per year. You pay a monthly premium for the supplement, but in return, you get peace of mind with a nearly unlimited choice of doctors anywhere in the country and no networks or referrals required.

- **Medicare Advantage (Part C) plans:** These "all-in-one" plans replace Original Medicare and are offered by private companies approved by Medicare. Most include Part D drug coverage plus extra benefits such as routine dental, vision, hearing aids, or even gym memberships. They come with an annual out-of-pocket maximum (often $5,000–$10,000, depending on the plan in 2026), set copays instead of unlimited 20% coinsurance, and built-in limits on what you pay each year. Many plans have an additional premium of $0, in addition to your Part B premium.

Both options provide protection that Original Medicare alone cannot. The best choice for you depends on your health needs, budget, the doctors you prefer, how much you travel, and whether you like the flexibility of any provider or the extras that come with many Advantage plans.

Why This Matters for You

I see this situation often with clients: People sign up for Original Medicare thinking it will be "enough," only to receive a large, unexpected bill later. The good news is that adding a Medicare Supplement or enrolling in a Medicare Advantage plan early can protect your savings and give you real peace of mind when you need care most.

In the coming chapters, we'll explore Medigap plans in detail, including the most popular ones, such as Plan G and Plan N, and how to compare them. You'll gain clear, practical guidance so you can choose the option that best fits your health, your budget, and your lifestyle.

Original Medicare alone is a starting point, not a finish line. The next two chapters show you how to cross it.

65

Chapter 9

Medicare Supplement Insurance (Medigap)

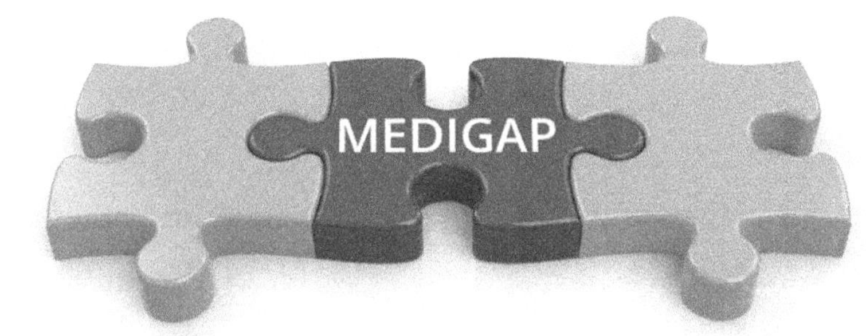

Now that you understand the foundation of Original Medicare and the gaps that can leave you with unexpected costs, let's talk about one of the most popular ways to get stronger protection: Medicare Supplement Plans, also known as Medigap.

Medicare Supplement Plans (Medigap) policies are private insurance plans designed to work alongside Original Medicare (Parts A and B). They help pay the deductibles, coinsurance, and copays that Original Medicare leaves behind. Think of them as a safety net that makes your out-of-pocket costs much more predictable and manageable.

How Medicare Supplement Plans (Medigap) Work

You must have Original Medicare (both Part A and Part B) to buy a Medicare Supplement Plan (Medigap) policy. The supplement then pays a portion, or in many cases, nearly all of the costs that Original Medicare does not cover.

Medigap plans are standardized by the government and labeled with letters (A, B, C, D, F, G, K, L, M, and N). Each letter offers a different level of coverage. The benefits are exactly the same, no matter which insurance company sells the plan. Only the monthly premium changes from company to company.

The Most Popular Medigap Plans in 2026

Here are the plans I recommend most often to clients:
- **Plan G**: The most comprehensive option available to new Medicare beneficiaries. It covers Part A deductible, all Part A and Part B coinsurance and copays, excess charges, and foreign travel emergencies. You usually pay only the annual Part B deductible ($283 in 2026) out of pocket. This plan gives you excellent protection and nationwide flexibility to see any doctor who accepts Medicare.

- **High-Deductible G:** High-Deductible G works the same as Plan G; however, it has a deductible of $2,950 that you must meet before the plan starts paying.
- **Plan N:** A slightly more affordable alternative to Plan G. It covers most of the same benefits but requires you to pay small copays for doctor visits and emergency room visits. It does not cover the Part B deductible or excess charges. Many clients choose Plan N because the lower monthly premium fits their budget while still providing strong coverage.
- **Plan F:** Once the gold standard, but it is no longer available to people who became eligible for Medicare after January 1, 2020. If you were eligible before that date and already have Plan F, you can keep it.

Other plans like K, L, and M offer more limited coverage and are chosen less often because they still result in higher costs.

Key Benefits Most Medigap Plans Provide:

- Coverage of the Part A hospital deductible, 20% coinsurance, and copays

- Coverage of the Part B 20% coinsurance and copays for doctor visits and outpatient services
- Skilled nursing facility coinsurance (Days 21–100)
- Hospice care coinsurance and copayments
- The first three pints of blood each year
- Foreign travel emergency coverage (up to 80% after a $250 deductible, up to $50,000 lifetime limit)

With a Medigap policy, there are no networks and no referrals required. You can see any doctor or specialist who accepts Medicare anywhere in the United States without prior authorization. Combined with Original Medicare, a Medigap plan can cover most or all of your out-of-pocket costs, giving you maximum predictability and peace of mind.

Costs of Medigap Plans

You pay a monthly premium for your Medigap policy in addition to your Part B premium. Premiums vary by:
- Your age, gender, and location
- Whether you use tobacco
- The insurance provider you choose.
- The specific plan letter (G usually costs more than N)

In 2026, a typical Plan G premium for a 65-year-old might range from $120 to $250 per month, depending on where you live, gender, and your health habits. Plan N is over time, but they are usually more stable than paying unpredictable coinsurance bills.

Real Life Examples

1.   John has a 10-day hospital stay followed by several doctor visits and outpatient tests. With only Original Medicare, he would pay $1,736 Part A deductible, copays, plus 20% coinsurance on all services. With a Plan G supplement, he pays only the $283 Part B deductible; everything else is covered.

2.   Maria needs ongoing specialist care and physical therapy. The 20% coinsurance can add up to several thousand dollars per year under Original Medicare alone. Her Plan N keeps her costs low with small copays instead of unlimited 20% coinsurance.

These examples show why so many people say their Medigap plan is "worth every penny" when they actually need care.

Common Questions About Medigap

- **When is the best time to buy?** The best time is during your 6-month Medigap Open Enrollment Period, which begins the month you turn 65 and/or you enroll in Part B. During this time, insurance companies cannot deny you coverage or charge more because of pre-existing conditions.
- **Can I be turned down later?** After the open enrollment period, companies can ask health questions and may deny coverage or charge higher rates if you have health issues.
- **Do I still need Prescription Coverage?** Yes. Medigap does not cover prescription drugs, so you will still need a separate prescription plan, known as a Part D plan.

Checklist: Deciding If Medigap Is Right for You

- You want to see any Medicare-accepting doctor without networks or referrals.
- You prefer predictable monthly costs instead of variable coinsurance.
- You are willing to pay a monthly premium for maximum protection.

- You have or are expecting serious health issues in the future.
- You travel frequently.

As long as you pay your monthly premium, your Medigap policy is Guaranteed Renewable. This means it is automatically renewed each year regardless of changes in your health status.

Medigap turns Medicare's biggest financial risks into predictable, manageable costs. That's not just coverage; that's peace of mind with a price tag you can plan around.

In the next chapter, we'll put real numbers behind that peace of mind. You'll see exactly what Original Medicare costs in premiums, deductibles, and out-of-pocket expenses are, so you can begin building a clear picture of what Medicare will actually mean for your budget.

Chapter 10

Crunching the Numbers

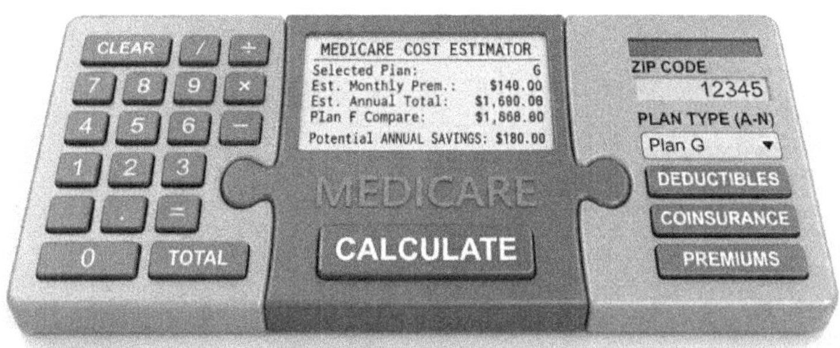

Understanding Medicare costs is one of the most important parts of planning your coverage. While Original Medicare provides strong protection, premiums, deductibles, coinsurance, and copays can add up, especially without extra safeguards. However, options like Medigap plans or Medicare Advantage plans can help cap your spending and bring real predictability to your budget.

In this chapter, we'll break down the main 2026 costs for Original Medicare (Parts A and B), prescription drug coverage (Part D or included in Medicare Advantage), and Medicare Advantage plans overall. You'll also get practical, battle-tested tips to help you lower costs and protect your savings.

Original Medicare Costs (Parts A and B)

Most people qualify for premium-free Part A, but Part B always has a monthly premium.

Part A (Hospital Insurance):

- **Premium**: $0 for most people (if you or your spouse paid Medicare taxes for 10+ years). If you don't have enough work credits, the monthly premium is $311 (reduced rate) or up to $565.
- **Inpatient Hospital Deductible**: $1,736 per benefit period.
- **Hospital Copays**: $0 for days 1–60 (after deductible); $434 per day for days 61–90; $868 per day for lifetime reserve days (only 60 over your lifetime); 100% of costs after that.
- **Hospital Coinsurance**: The plan pays 80%, and you pay 20% for all covered services.
- **Skilled Nursing Copays**: $0 for days 1–20 (after a qualifying 3-day hospital stay); $217 per day for days 21–100; 100% of costs after that.
- **Hospice**: Small copays for outpatient drugs and 5% coinsurance for inpatient respite care; room and board usually not covered.
- **No Maximum Out-of-Pocket:** There is no maximum out-of-pocket limit.

Real Life Example

> *John has a heart attack and is staying in the hospital for 5 days. He pays a $1,736 deductible once per benefit period, plus any applicable coinsurance. Medicare then covers the rest for those days. Knowing these numbers ahead of time helps families plan and reduces stress during unexpected health events.*

Part B (Medical Insurance) Costs:

- **Monthly Premium**: It is usually deducted directly from Social Security.
- **Annual Deductible**: Paid once per calendar year.
- **Copays**: Can range from $0 - $45 plus, depending on the situation.
- **Coinsurance**: Typically, 20% of the Medicare-approved amount after the deductible for doctor visits, outpatient care, durable medical equipment, and most services. Many preventive services are $0.
- **No Maximum Out-of-Pocket:** There is no maximum out-of-pocket limit.
- **Late Enrollment Penalty**: 10% is added to your Part B premium for every 12 months you delay enrollment.
- **IRMAA**: A surcharge that higher-income beneficiaries must pay.

Real Life Example

> *Sarah goes for her annual wellness visit and a mammogram screening. Both are preventive, so she pays nothing. Later, she sees her doctor for a routine checkup and pays the yearly deductible if it hasn't been met yet. Then, she pays copay and 20 percent coinsurance on the approved amount. These everyday examples show how Part B helps keep you healthy without surprise bills for routine care.*

Part C (Medicare Advantage) Costs:

These all-in-one plans replace Original Medicare's cost-sharing with their own rules and usually include drug coverage plus extras like dental, vision, and hearing.

- **Monthly Premium**: Many plans have a $0 additional premium (you still pay your Part B premium, which may include IRMAA).
- **Deductibles, Copays, and Coinsurance**: Fixed amounts that vary by plan—often more predictable than Original Medicare's 20%.
- **Annual Out-of-Pocket Maximum**: Varies by plan, but the Medicare maximum is $9,250 for in-network services in 2026 (some plans set it much lower). Once you hit it, you pay $0 for covered medical services for the rest of the year. Keep in

mind, your drug costs have their own separate maximum out-of-pocket cap.

Real Life Example

Mike chooses a Medicare Advantage HMO plan with a $0 premium. It covers his regular doctor visits, including dental cleanings twice a year, and caps his yearly out-of-pocket costs at $6,700. For many people, this combination of extras and a spending limit brings real peace of mind.

Part D (Prescription Drug) Costs:

Thanks to the Inflation Reduction Act, the 2026 structure is much simpler, with a clear $2,100 out-of-pocket cap on covered drugs.

- **Monthly Premium**: The average Part D Standalone premium is around $34.50. Many Medicare Advantage plans include drug coverage with $0 or incredibly low additional premiums.
- **Deductible**: Up to $615 (many plans' deductibles are less or sometimes even 0$).
- **Copays/Coinsurance**: Vary by drug tier; often low fixed copays for generics ($0–$10). Brand names typically are more expensive. You pay until you hit the cap.

- **Annual Out-of-Pocket Cap**: $2,100 for covered drugs on the plan's formulary. Once you reach it, you pay $0 for covered prescriptions for the rest of the year.
- **Insulin**: Capped at $35 per month for covered insulin products.
- **Vaccines**: Most recommended vaccines (shingles, flu, etc.) are $0.
- **Late Enrollment Penalty**: 1% of the National Base Beneficiary Premium is assessed for every month delayed.
- **IRMAA**: A surcharge that higher-income beneficiaries must pay.

Real Life Example

Linda takes several medications for blood pressure and cholesterol. Her Part D plan covers them with modest copays of $10–$50 per month. After she spends $2,100 out-of-pocket on covered drugs, the plan pays 100% for the rest of the year. This cap protects people who need ongoing prescriptions from facing unlimited costs.

What Is IRMAA?

IRMAA stands for **Income-Related Monthly Adjustment Amount**. It is an extra surcharge that higher-income Medicare beneficiaries must pay on top of their standard Part B and Part D premiums.

The Social Security Administration determines IRMAA based on your **modified adjusted gross income (MAGI)** from your federal tax return **two years earlier**. For 2026 premiums, they look at your 2024 tax return.

- If your 2024 income was $109,000 or less (individual) or $218,000 or less (married filing jointly), you pay only the standard premiums.
- If your income was higher, you pay the standard premium plus an IRMAA surcharge.
- This applies whether you have Original Medicare or a Medicare Advantage plan.

IRMAA affects roughly 8% of beneficiaries, and the surcharges are set on a sliding scale. The good news is that if your income has dropped significantly (due to retirement, divorce, loss of a spouse, or other life-changing events), you can file an appeal (Form SSA-44) to request a lower amount using more recent income information. Many have successfully reduced or eliminated their IRMAA this way.

2026 Part B IRMAA Table (based on 2024 MAGI):

Filing Status	2024 Income Thresholds	IRMAA Surcharge	Total Monthly Premium
Individual / Joint	≤$109,000 / ≤$218,000	$0	$202.90
Individual / Joint	>$109,000 - ≤$137,000 / >$218,000 - ≤$274,000	$81.20	$284.10
Individual / Joint	>$137,000 - ≤$171,000 / >$274,000 - ≤$342,000	$202.90	$405.80
Individual / Joint	>$171,000 - ≤$205,000 / >$342,000 - ≤$410,000	$324.60	$527.50
Individual / Joint	>$205,000 - ≤$500,000 / >$410,000 - ≤$750,000	$446.30	$649.20
Individual / Joint	≥$500,000 / ≥$750,000	$487.00	$689.90

(Married filing separately has different brackets—often higher surcharges. Check your Social Security notice or call 1-800-772-1213 for your exact amount.)

IRMAA Surcharge for Part D: Added to your plan premium if your 2024 income exceeds the thresholds (same brackets as Part B). Surcharges range from $14.50 to $91.00 per month, depending on your income tier.

Savings Tips to Lower Your Medicare Costs

Here are the exact strategies to keep expenses manageable:

1. Secure premium-free Part A if you (or your spouse) have enough work credits.
2. Enroll on time to avoid lifelong late penalties.
3. Compare plans **every year** during the Annual Election Period (Oct 15 to Dec 7).
4. Use generics, preferred pharmacies, and mail-order to slash prescription costs.
5. Apply for **Extra Help** (Low-Income Subsidy) if eligible—it can eliminate or dramatically reduce Part D premiums and out-of-pocket costs.
6. Add a strong Medigap plan like Plan G for near-zero out-of-pocket costs on Original Medicare (after the $283 Part B deductible).
7. Consider a Medicare Advantage plan if you want built-in spending caps, extra benefits, and often lower monthly premiums.
8. Appeal your IRMAA if your income has decreased—many clients save hundreds per year this way.

9. Take full advantage of $0 preventive services under Part B to catch any health issues early.
10. Use the Medicare Prescription Payment Plan to spread drug costs evenly throughout the year.

Medicare costs become far more predictable once you understand them and pick the right combination of coverage. With the right setup, you can keep expenses low even as your health needs change over time.

In the next chapter, we'll cover enrolling without penalties, when and how to sign up or make changes, so you never pay extra.

Truth is in the numbers! Taking time now to crunch these numbers helps you make confident, budget-friendly decisions for the years ahead.

Chapter 11

Enrolling Without Penalties

Signing up for Medicare does not have to be complicated. Knowing the right time to enroll helps you start your coverage smoothly, avoid penalties, and choose the options that best fit your health and budget. Most people become eligible at age 65, and the process is straightforward, especially when you plan a few months in advance.

In this chapter, we'll walk through the main enrollment periods for 2026, when your coverage actually starts, the late penalties to watch out for, and simple ways to complete the process. The goal is to get you covered without gaps or extra costs so you can focus on what matters most, your health and peace of mind.

Key Enrollment Periods

Medicare has specific windows for signing up or making changes. Here are the most important ones you need to know:

Initial Enrollment Period (IEP)

This is your first and best opportunity to enroll. It usually begins three months before the month you turn 65, includes your birthday month, and lasts three months after, for a total of seven months.

- If your birthday falls on the first of the month, the period starts four months before your birthday month and ends two months after.
- Signing up in the first three months of your IEP usually means coverage starts on the first day of your birthday month.
- If you are already receiving Social Security benefits, Part A often starts automatically, and Part B may be started as well (you can opt out of Part B if you have other qualifying coverage).

Enrolling during your IEP is especially important because it also opens a six-month Medicare Supplement Plans (Medigap) Open Enrollment Period. During this time, insurance companies cannot deny you a Medigap plan or charge you more because of pre-existing conditions.

Annual Election Period (AEP)

Every year from October 15 to December 7. This is the main time when anyone with Medicare can make changes for the following year:

- Join, switch, or drop a Medicare Advantage plan (with or without drug coverage).
- Join, switch, or drop a standalone Part D drug plan.
- Switch from Medicare Advantage back to Original Medicare (or the other way around).

Any changes you make during this period take effect on January 1 of the next year. This is your annual chance to review your coverage and ensure it still meets your needs.

Medicare Advantage Open Enrollment Period (MA OEP)

January 1 to March 31 each year. If you are already enrolled in a Medicare Advantage plan, you can make one change during this period: switch to a different Medicare Advantage plan or return to Original Medicare (and add a Part D plan if needed). Changes usually start the first day of the following month.

Special Enrollment Periods (SEP)

These allow you to enroll or make changes outside the regular windows if you experience a qualifying life event, such as:

- Losing employer group health coverage (from an employer with 20 or more employees) or creditable drug coverage.
- Moving to a new area outside your current plan's service region.
- Gaining or losing Medicaid, Extra Help, or other qualifying coverage.
- Your plan is ending its contract with Medicare or making major changes.
- Enabling your one-time Medicare Advantage Trial Right with a less than 12-month-old Medicare Advantage plan.

In 2026, a new SEP also applies if you enrolled in a Medicare Advantage plan based on incorrect network information from Medicare's online tools. Most SEPs last two months (or up to eight months in certain employer coverage situations), and coverage can often begin sooner than during the General Enrollment Period.

General Enrollment Period (GEP)

If you miss your Initial Enrollment Period and do not qualify for a Special Enrollment Period, you can sign up from January 1 to March 31 each year. Coverage will start the month after you enroll, but you may face a Part B and Part D late enrollment penalty.

Avoiding Penalties

Late penalties can increase your premiums for the rest of your life, so it's important to enroll on time:

- **Part B Late Penalty:** 10% added to your monthly premium for each full 12-month period you were eligible for Part B but did not enroll (unless you had qualifying employer coverage).
- **Part D Late Penalty:** Approximately 1% of the national base cost added to your premium for each month you delayed enrollment without creditable drug coverage.

The simplest way to avoid both penalties is to enroll during your Initial Enrollment Period or use a Special Enrollment Period when you qualify.

How to Sign Up: Simple Steps

Enrolling is easier than most people expect. Here are the most common ways:

- **Online:** The fastest option for most people. Visit www.ssa.gov to apply for Parts A and B or use Medicare.gov/plan-compare to shop for Medicare Advantage or Part D plans.
- **By Phone:** Call Social Security at 1-800-772-1213 or 1-800-MEDICARE (1-800-633-4227) for help with plans.
- **In Person:** Visit your local Social Security office (appointments are recommended).
- **Through a Broker:** Contact an independent, trusted Medicare broker. They should offer free, no-obligation help comparing plans, checking eligibility, and handling the enrollment paperwork. Working with a broker costs you nothing, and they can explain every option tailored to your situation.

If you are already receiving Social Security benefits, Parts A and B often start automatically when you turn 65. Otherwise, apply within three months before your birthday month to ensure a smooth transition of coverage.

Quick Tips for Success

- Gather your documents ahead of time: Social Security number, birth certificate or passport, and details about any employer coverage.
- Check whether you will be automatically enrolled if you're already on Social Security.
- Start reviewing your options early, as plans and costs can change every year.

Getting your Medicare enrollment right sets the foundation for a smooth experience. When you enroll on time and choose coverage that fits your needs, you avoid penalties and enjoy better protection and lower stress for years to come.

In the next chapter, we'll explore costly mistakes and how to avoid them.

Timing is everything! Planning your enrollment now gives you confidence and control over your Medicare journey.

Chapter 12

Costly Mistakes

Turning 65 or becoming Medicare-eligible should bring peace of mind, not financial stress. Yet every year, thousands of Americans make honest mistakes during enrollment or plan selection, resulting in permanent premium penalties, surprise medical bills, or coverage gaps that can cost tens of thousands of dollars over time.

This chapter highlights the most common and expensive mistakes so that you can avoid them with confidence.

Mistake #1: Missing or Mishandling Your Initial Enrollment Period (IEP)

Your seven-month IEP begins three months before your 65th birthday month, includes your birthday month, and ends three months after. This is your penalty-free window to enroll in Medicare Parts A and B (and Part D).

Delaying Part B enrollment without qualifying for creditable coverage (such as employer group health insurance from a company with 20+ employees) equals a permanent late enrollment penalty of 10% added to your Part B premium for each full 12-month period you waited. In 2026, the standard Part B premium is $202.90 per month. A two-year delay adds a 20% penalty, increasing your monthly premium by about $40.58, which you will have to pay for the rest of your life.

Delay Part D enrollment (or a Medicare Advantage plan with drug coverage) without creditable prescription coverage results in a lifelong penalty of 1% of the national base beneficiary premium ($38.99 in 2026) for every month you lack coverage. This penalty will be added to your monthly premium and recalculated every year.

Real Life Example

Mike, a retiree, thought his former employer's retiree plan covered everything. He enrolled in Medicare eight months late and now pays an extra $50+ every month on Part B and Part D penalties for the rest of his life. This amounts to over $15,000 in extra costs over 25 years.

How to avoid it: Mark your calendar with your exact IEP dates at least four months before the 1st day of your birth month. If you're still working with qualifying employer coverage, get written confirmation that it is "creditable." 1

Mistake #2: Assuming Medicare Is Free

Many people are surprised to learn that while Part A is often premium-free, Part B carries a monthly premium. Higher-income beneficiaries may also pay IRMAA surcharges.

How to avoid it: Budget for premiums, deductibles, copays, and 20% coinsurance. Use tools such as Medicare.gov to get a clear cost projection based on your situation.

Mistake #3: Choosing a Plan Based Only on Premium (or on What Worked for Someone Else)

The lowest premium Medicare Advantage or Part D plan may have higher copays, a restricted doctor network, or poor coverage for your specific medications. What's perfect for your neighbor may not be perfect for you. Imitating their coverage could leave you paying more or losing access to your preferred doctors.

How to avoid it: Always compare total estimated annual costs (premium + deductible + copays + coinsurance) using your actual doctors and current prescription list. Never choose based on a friend's recommendation alone.

Mistake #4: Skipping Your Annual Review

Medicare Advantage plans and Part D formularies can change every year. Networks shrink, drugs can change tiers within the formulary, and premiums rise. Automatically renewing can increase your costs or disrupt your care.

How to avoid it: Treat the Annual Election Period (October 15 to December 7) as mandatory "homework." Review your Annual Notice of Change (ANOC) letter from your planned provider and compare options every year. A quick check can save hundreds or even thousands of dollars.

Mistake #5: Not Understanding the Fundamental Difference Between Medicare Advantage (Part C) and Medigap

Medicare Advantage replaces Original Medicare with a private plan (often bundles Part D and extras and may include networks and prior authorizations).

Medigap works alongside Original Medicare to help cover deductibles and coinsurance, giving you freedom to see any doctor who accepts Medicare.

Switching paths later can be difficult and trigger health questions and underwriting.

How to avoid it: Decide early which route best fits your health needs, travel plans, and budget. Ensure that you compare plans across all carriers side by side.

Mistake #6: Thinking "I Don't Take Many Medications Now, So I'll Skip Part D"

Prescription needs often change with age or new diagnoses. Enrolling late triggers the Part D penalty, and you could face both the penalty and much higher drug costs when you need coverage most.

How to avoid it: Secure creditable drug coverage during your IEP (Initial Enrollment Period), even if your current medications are inexpensive.

Mistake #7: Overlooking Special Enrollment Periods or Equitable Relief

Life events (losing coverage, moving, or even certain mistakes by Social Security) can create penalty-free windows. Many people miss them or fail to document everything properly.

How to avoid it: Keep records of all communications. If a government representative gave you incorrect information, ask about potentially obtaining equitable relief to waive a penalty.

Your Action Steps to Stay Protected

- Calculate and calendar your exact Initial Enrollment Period today.
- Gather your doctor list and current prescriptions.
- Schedule a no-obligation Medicare review with an independent broker who can compare real options for your situation.
- Mark next year's Annual Election Period on your calendar now.

You have worked hard to reach this stage. Don't let a preventable mistake erode what you've built. Master these pitfalls, and you will enjoy Medicare with confidence and financial security.

In the next chapter, we will cover special situations that may be unique to your situation. The mistakes in this chapter cost real people real money. You now have everything you need to make sure none of them cost you. Forewarned is forearmed. You are ready!

Chapter 13

Special Situations

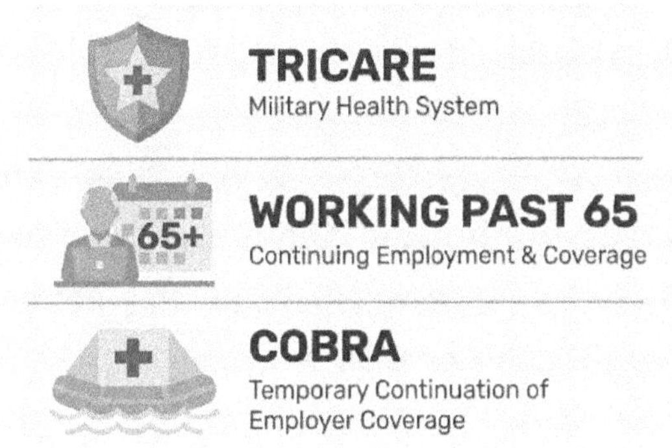

Medicare does not exist in a vacuum. Many people have other insurance through a current job, a spouse's employer, retiree benefits, or programs like TRICARE, VA, or FEHB. Knowing exactly how Medicare coordinates with these other plans is crucial to avoid coverage gaps, late penalties, or unexpected costs. The rules depend on several factors, including the employer's size, whether you are still actively employed, and the specific type of coverage you have.

In this chapter, we will walk through the most common scenarios for 2026: working past age 65 with employer-sponsored group health coverage, retiree plans, and COBRA, as well as general coordination rules for other types of insurance. Understanding these situations will help you make confident decisions and keep your coverage seamless.

Working Past 65 with Employer Group Health Coverage

If you or your spouse is still actively working and covered by an employer group health plan, you often have the option to delay enrolling in Medicare Parts B and D without facing penalties. Part A (hospital insurance) is usually premium-free and may still be worth enrolling in at age 65 for added protection.

The key factor is the size of the employer (based on the number of employees):

- **Employers with 20 or more employees:** The creditable group health plan pays first as the primary payer, and Medicare pays second as the secondary payer for covered services. In this situation, you can safely delay Part B enrollment during your Initial Enrollment Period without a late penalty. Many people in larger companies choose to skip Part B at age 65 to avoid the monthly premium because their employer-sponsored creditable plan already covers most of their needs. Your employer is required to offer the same benefits to employees age 65 and older as it does to younger workers.

- **Employers with fewer than 20 employees:** Medicare pays first as the primary payer, and the group plan pays second (or may not pay much at all). In this case, it is usually best to enroll in both Parts A and B at age 65 to avoid gaps or penalties. Many small-employer plans actually require Medicare enrollment and will only coordinate as secondary coverage.

The same rules generally apply if the coverage comes through your spouse's employer. Always confirm the details directly with your benefits administrator. Ask these key questions:

- Is the plan "creditable" (at least as good as Medicare for Parts A & B plus Part D) so you can delay without penalty?
- How will claims be processed once Medicare is involved?
- Will enrolling in Medicare affect your dependents or the ability to contribute to an HSA? (You must stop HSA contributions once you enroll in any part of Medicare.)

When you eventually retire or lose the group coverage, you will qualify for a Special Enrollment Period to sign up for Parts A, B, and D without penalties. Coverage can begin the month after you enroll (or sooner in some cases), so it is wise to sign up a month or two before your employer plan ends to prevent any gap in coverage.

Retiree Coverage and COBRA

Retiree health plans from a former employer and COBRA continuation coverage follow different rules than active employee plans.

- **Retiree Coverage:** Medicare usually pays first as the primary payer, and the retiree plan pays second. Many retiree plans require you to enroll in Medicare Parts A and B in order to keep or maximize their benefits. Carefully check your plan documents. Some retiree benefits only function as a supplement to Medicare. Skipping Part B could leave you responsible for high costs or even cause you to lose the retiree coverage altogether. Be especially cautious about joining a Medicare Advantage plan without confirming it will not affect your retiree benefits.
- **COBRA:** If you elect COBRA after leaving a job or retiring, Medicare generally **pays first**, and COBRA pays second. Important note: Most of the time, COBRA does **not** count as creditable coverage for delaying Part B or Part D penalties.

Confirm directly with your plan administrator or with Social Security. You should enroll in Medicare A, B, and D during your Special Enrollment Period. COBRA can continue alongside Medicare, but it may terminate if you enroll in Medicare after electing COBRA.

In both cases, contact your former employer's benefits administrator before making any changes. Some plans coordinate smoothly with Medicare, while others may reduce or end benefits if you do not enroll correctly.

Other Common Coordination Situations

- **TRICARE, CHAMPVA, VA, or FEHB (Federal Employees/Retirees):** Rules vary by program. For most, Medicare pays first, but TRICARE and VA benefits may coordinate differently depending on your status. FEHB plans often become secondary after you enroll in Medicare.

- **Medicaid or Dual Eligibility:** Medicare pays first as the primary payer; Medicaid covers many of the remaining costs.

- **Workers' Compensation, No-Fault, or Liability Insurance:** These usually pay first for any claims related to an injury or accident.

In every situation, the primary payer covers its limits first, then the secondary payer steps in for any remaining approved costs (though it may not cover everything). Providers are required to bill the primary payer first.

Tips for Handling Coordination Smoothly

- Talk to your employer's HR or benefits administrator early and ask for written details about coordination rules, creditable status, and how enrolling in Medicare will affect your coverage.
- Use Medicare.gov or call 1-800-MEDICARE to verify the exact rules for your specific situation.
- If you are planning to retire soon, start the Medicare enrollment process before your Special Enrollment Period so you avoid any gaps in coverage.

These coordination situations can feel overwhelming at first, but getting them right saves money and ensures you have seamless care when you need it.

In the next chapter, we will look at how to put it all together. You will see how to compare your options and choose the coverage that best fits your needs.

The pieces are coming together! Understanding how Medicare works with your other insurance gives you control and confidence for the years ahead.

Chapter 14

Medicare Advantage vs. Medicare Supplement (Medigap)

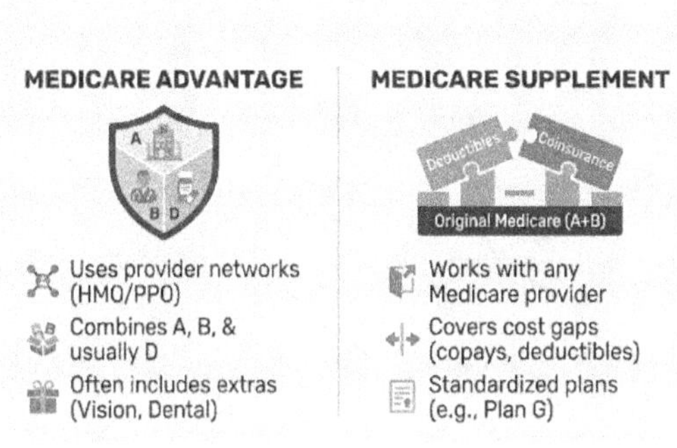

One of the most important and often most confusing decisions you will face once you begin your Medicare journey is whether to enroll in a Medicare Advantage (Part C) plan or stay with Original Medicare plus a Medicare Supplement (Medigap) policy.

This single choice can dramatically affect your monthly premiums, your out-of-pocket costs, which doctors you can see, how your prescriptions are covered, and even how much peace of mind you have each year. Neither option is universally better for everyone. The right path depends entirely on your current and future health needs, your budget, the doctors, and hospitals you prefer, your travel habits, how many prescriptions you take, and how much certainty you want in your healthcare expenses.

As a Medicare broker, I have guided thousands of beneficiaries nationwide through this exact comparison. Some people thrive with the extra benefits and lower premiums of Medicare Advantage, while others find true security with the broad flexibility and predictable costs of Medigap. This chapter breaks everything down clearly, shows you a side-by-side visual comparison, and provides a practical decision checklist so you can move forward with confidence instead of second-guessing your coverage.

How the Two Options Actually Work

Medicare Advantage (Part C) plans are private insurance plans approved by Medicare. When you choose a Medicare Advantage Plan, it replaces your Original Medicare coverage. Please note, you must still be enrolled in Original Medicare. These plans are required to cover at least everything Original Medicare covers, but most go further by bundling in prescription drug coverage (Part D) and adding popular extra benefits such as routine dental, vision, hearing aids, fitness programs, and even transportation to doctor visits.

Medigap works differently. You remain enrolled in Original Medicare (Parts A and B), and you purchase a standardized supplement policy from a private insurance company. The Medigap policy is designed specifically to "fill the gaps" in Original Medicare by helping pay deductibles, coinsurance, and copayments. Because

Medigap does not include prescription drugs, you will need a separate, standalone Part D plan.

Important Rule: You cannot have both a Medicare Advantage plan and a Medigap policy at the same time. Once you choose one path, the other is no longer an option unless you disenroll and return to Original Medicare during an allowable period.

Side-by-Side Comparison (2026)

Category	Medicare Advantage (Part C)	Original Medicare + Medigap
Doctors & Hospitals	Usually limited to the plan's network (HMO or PPO). Out-of-network care may cost more or not be covered at all.	You can see any doctor or go to any hospital that accepts Medicare. This is nationwide and gives freedom of choice with no network restrictions.
Referrals & Prior Authorizations	Often required for specialists and many services, such as surgeries or advanced imaging.	No referrals needed; prior approvals are rarely required.
Monthly Premiums (in addition to the standard Part B premium	Often **$0** or very low (national average around $14–$17), though some plans do charge more.	Typically, **$120–$250+** per month for the popular Plan G, depending on your age, gender, health habits, and location.

Category	Medicare Advantage (Part C)	Original Medicare + Medigap
Out-of-Pocket Costs	Deductibles, copays, and coinsurance may apply per service; however, there is an annual out-of-pocket maximum of **$9,250** for in-network.	Very predictable. After the Part B deductible, you usually pay little to no coinsurance or copays (especially with Plan G or Plan F, where they are still available).
Prescription Drugs Monthly Premiums	Usually included (most are MA-PD plans).	Not included. It requires a separate, standalone Part D plan.
Extra Benefits	Often includes routine dental cleanings and procedures, vision exams and eyewear, hearing aids, gym memberships, over-the-counter allowances, and transportation.	None. It provides pure gap coverage only.
Travel & Snowbirds	Coverage is usually limited to the plan's service area; out-of-area care is often restricted to emergencies only.	Full coverage anywhere in the U.S., wherever Medicare is accepted, plus limited foreign travel emergency benefits on most plans.
Best For	Healthier individuals who want lower premiums, extra benefits, and are comfortable staying within a network.	People who see specialists often, travel frequently, value maximum doctor choice, or want highly predictable costs year after year.

Decision Checklist: Which Plan Wins for You?

Take a moment to answer these questions honestly.

- Do you see specialists regularly or manage one or more ongoing health conditions?
    - Medigap usually provides more flexibility and cost predictability.
- Are you relatively healthy right now and mainly interested in preventive care plus attractive extras like dental and vision?
    - Medicare Advantage may save you money upfront and give you more value.
- Do you travel often or live a snowbird lifestyle, splitting time between different states?
    - Medigap typically offers far better nationwide protection.
- Is keeping your monthly premium as low as possible more important to you than knowing exactly what your total costs will be each year?
    - Low premium = Medicare Advantage
    - Predictable costs = Medigap
- Would you prefer to carry just one easy insurance card that covers hospital, medical, and prescription drugs?
    - Medicare Advantage is usually simpler in that regard.

- Are you comfortable with the possibility of changing doctors or plans if the network changes in the future?
    - Think carefully before choosing Medicare Advantage.
- What would your budget look like if you faced a serious health event in a given year?
    - Medicare Advantage has a maximum out-of-pocket cap; Medigap keeps your per-service costs very low with almost no surprises.

Real Talk from a Medicare Broker

In my experience working with beneficiaries across the country, many people are initially drawn to Medicare Advantage because of the low or $0 monthly premiums and the appealing extra benefits. They enjoy the added perks until they need frequent specialist care or want to see a provider who is outside the plan's network. At that point, copays and coinsurance costs can add up quickly, and the limited flexibility can be frustrating.

On the other hand, those who choose Medigap often tell me they sleep much better at night. They know their costs are locked in, they can see virtually any doctor who accepts Medicare, and they don't have to worry about network changes or prior authorizations. The trade-off is usually a higher monthly premium.

There is no single "winner" in this comparison. The best plan is simply the one that matches your lifestyle, your health reality, and the kind of security you want for the years ahead.

Next Steps

- Make a list of your current doctors, medications, and any travel plans for the coming year.
- Spend time comparing specific plans side by side on Medicare.gov or with an independent broker.
- Schedule a no-obligation Medicare review with a trusted advisor who represents multiple carriers so you can see real quotes tailored to you.

In the next chapter, we'll move on to mastering your Medicare choices, so you can confidently evaluate every available path and build a strategy that serves you well for years to come.

You deserve Medicare coverage that truly fits your life, and now you have what it takes to find it!

Chapter 15

Mastering Your Medicare Choices

Now that you understand the building blocks of Medicare and have seen a clear head-to-head comparison between Medicare Advantage and Original Medicare, plus a Medicare Supplement (Medigap) policy. The next important step is turning that knowledge into a confident choice that fits your life today and for years to come.

Medicare is not one-size-fits-all. The best coverage for you depends on your current and expected health needs, your budget, your preferred doctors, your medications, your travel habits, and how much predictability you want in your spending.

Step 1: Assess Your Personal Situation

Take a few minutes to answer these honest questions and jot down your answers. This becomes your personal decision-making guide:

- What are your current and expected health needs? Do you see specialists often, manage chronic conditions, or expect more care in the coming years?
- What is your comfort level with monthly premiums versus potential out-of-pocket costs during a major health event?
- How important is the ability to see any Medicare-accepting doctor or hospital nationwide?
- Do you travel frequently or live a snowbird lifestyle?
- Which extra benefits matter most to you right now: routine dental, vision, hearing aids, fitness programs, or transportation?
- Are you still working, have retiree coverage, or need to coordinate with other insurance?
- How important is predictable, low out-of-pocket spending versus keeping monthly premiums as low as possible?

Add your current medication list (with dosages) and your preferred doctors and pharmacies. Having this information written down makes every comparison much easier.

Step 2: Compare Your Options Practically

Now put real numbers to your situation:

- Use the official Medicare Plan Finder at Medicare.gov/plan-compare. Enter your ZIP code, medications, and doctors to see personalized estimates of premiums, deductibles, copays, and total yearly costs.
- Check networks carefully. Confirm your doctors are in-network for any Medicare Advantage plan you are considering.
- Review star ratings (aim for 4 or 5 stars) for plan quality and customer service.
- Calculate your estimated total annual cost: Add monthly premiums (Part B + any Medicare Supplement (Medigap) or Advantage premium + Part D) plus your expected deductibles, copays, and coinsurance based on how you actually use care.
- Run these comparisons during your Initial Enrollment Period or the Annual Election Period (October 15 to December 7). Feel free to compare

multiple times. Small changes in your health or medications can make a big difference.

Step 3: Plan Ahead and Review Every Year

Medicare is not a "set it and forget it" decision:

- Review your coverage every year during the Annual Enrollment Period because premiums, networks, formularies, and benefits can change.
- Watch for life events such as retirement, moving, changes in health, or income shifts that may affect IRMAA surcharges.
- If you are in a Medicare Advantage plan, you have an additional window from January 1 to March 31 to make a one-time per year plan change or return to Original Medicare.
- Keep good records of your choices, plan documents, and coverage details.
- Stay informed through Medicare.gov, 1-800-MEDICARE, or by working with a trusted independent Medicare broker who can alert you to important updates.

Final Thoughts on Choosing Wisely

There is no single perfect Medicare plan, only the one that best matches your life right now. Many people start with Original Medicare plus a Medicare Supplement (Medigap) for maximum flexibility and predictability. Others choose Medicare Advantage for lower premiums, extra benefits, and a built-in out-of-pocket maximum.

The key is to gather your personal information, compare the actual costs and trade-offs side by side, and make an informed choice you feel good about.

Taking the time to understand and compare your options now will give you stronger protection, lower stress, and greater peace of mind for many years to come.

In the next chapter, we will cover your rights, appeals, and how to fight a denial, so you know exactly what to do if something goes wrong.

There is no perfect plan, only the right plan for you. And now you know exactly how to find it.

Chapter 16

Your Rights, Appeals, and How to Fight a Denial

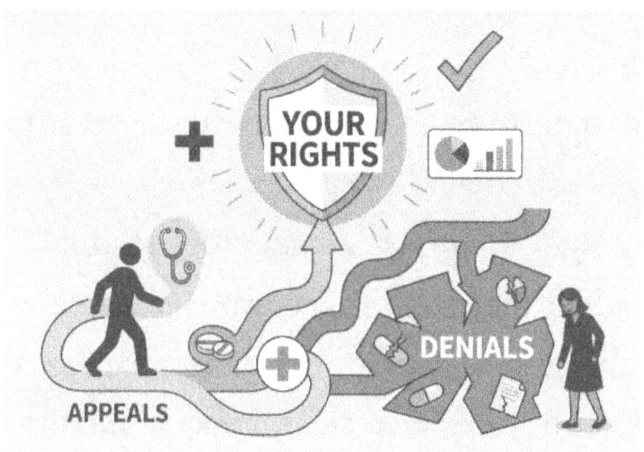

Medicare is a government program designed to protect your health and finances as you age, and federal laws give you strong rights and safeguards. Whether you have Original Medicare, a Medigap policy, a standalone Part D plan, or a Medicare Advantage plan, you have powerful protections against unfair treatment, wrongful denials, or poor service.

Most issues are resolved quickly once you know where to turn and how the system works. In this chapter, we will cover your core Medicare rights, key protections, the most common problems beneficiaries face, and a clear, step-by-step guide to effectively fighting a denial.

Knowing these rules puts you in control and helps you advocate for the coverage you deserve.

Your Core Medicare Rights

Medicare guarantees every beneficiary these fundamental protections:

- The right to receive all medical services that Medicare covers.
- The right to choose any doctor, hospital, or provider that accepts Medicare (with network rules applying in Medicare Advantage plans).
- The right to receive clear, understandable information about your coverage, costs, and any plan changes.
- The right to privacy and confidentiality of your personal health information (protected by HIPAA).
- The right to appeal any decision about coverage, payment, or services.
- The right to be treated with respect and without discrimination.
- The right to file complaints about the quality of care or how your plan operates.

You also have the right to switch plans during the Annual Election Period (October 15 to December 7) or other qualifying periods, usually without penalty.

Key Protections in Original Medicare and Medigap

Original Medicare (Parts A and B):
Medicare contractors handle coverage decisions. If a service is denied, you have well-defined appeal rights that can go through multiple levels of review.

Medigap: These policies are federally standardized. During your one-time 6-month Medigap Open Enrollment Period (which begins the month you turn 65 and enroll in Part B), insurance companies cannot deny you coverage, charge you more, or exclude pre-existing conditions based on your health. Outside this window, you may face medical underwriting unless you qualify for a guaranteed issue right, such as when you lose employer coverage, move out of a Medicare Advantage plan coverage area, or your plan is terminated.

Part D Prescription Drug Plans: Plans must cover drugs in protected classes (including treatments for cancer, HIV, epilepsy, and mental health). They must also consider exceptions and appeals if a drug is not on the formulary or requires prior authorization when it is medically necessary. Always check the plan's formulary to confirm your medications are covered, as lists vary by plan.

Key Protections in Medicare Advantage Plans

Medicare Advantage plans must follow strict federal rules, including:

- Medicare Advantage plans must cover the same services Original Medicare covers, though your cost sharing (copays, coinsurance) will follow the plans' own schedule rather than Original Medicare's rates.
- They are required to provide an annual out-of-pocket maximum.
- You have the right to a fast appeal if care is denied or terminated (for example, during a hospital discharge or home health services).
- Plans must give you at least 30 days' notice before making significant changes, such as reducing their provider network, and often more notice for premium increases.

If you become unhappy with your Medicare Advantage plan, you can usually switch back to Original Medicare during certain enrollment periods. Note that purchasing a

Medigap policy afterward may require answering health questions unless you qualify for guaranteed issue rights.

Step-by-Step: How to Fight a Denial

Here is a clear, practical process most beneficiaries can follow:

1. **Review the Denial Letter Carefully:** The letter will explain why the service was denied and outline your appeal rights, including exact deadlines. Keep this letter and all supporting documents.
2. **Gather Supporting Information:** Ask your doctor or provider for a detailed letter of medical necessity, medical records, or any additional evidence that shows why the service should be covered.
3. **File the First-Level Appeal:**
   - **Original Medicare**: Submit a request for redetermination to your Medicare Administrative Contractor (usually within 120 days).
   - **Medicare Advantage or Part D**: Follow the plan's internal appeal process. For urgent care, request a fast appeal (often decided within 72 hours).
4. **Escalate if Needed:** If the first level is denied, continue to higher levels: reconsideration by an

Independent Review Entity (IRE), then an Administrative Law Judge hearing, and beyond if necessary. Many appeals succeed when more complete medical information is provided.

5. **For Fast Appeals (Hospital Discharge or Ongoing Care):** Ask for a "Notice of Non-Coverage" or "Detailed Explanation of Non-Coverage." You have the right to a very quick review, which is often decided within 1 to 3 days, while care continues during the appeal.

Common Problems and Quick Solutions

- **Claim or Service Denial**: Start with the plan's or Medicare's appeal process as outlined above.
- **Billing Errors or Surprise Charges**: Contact the provider first to correct the bill. If unresolved, call 1-800-MEDICARE.
- **Problems with Your Plan (poor service, delayed authorizations, network issues)**: Call the plan directly. If not resolved, file a formal grievance with Medicare.
- **Fraud or Abuse (unsolicited sales calls, fake Medicare cards)**: Report immediately to 1-800-MEDICARE or the Senior Medicare Patrol at 1-877-808-2468. Never share personal information with unsolicited callers.

Resources for Help

- **1-800-MEDICARE (1-800-633-4227)**: Available 24/7 for questions, appeals guidance, and filing complaints.
- **Medicare.gov**: Use online tools to file appeals, submit complaints, and review your rights.

You have strong protections under Medicare law. Most problems are resolved successfully when you take prompt, informed action. Taking the time to understand your rights empowers you to protect your health and your wallet.

Next Steps

- Keep important Medicare documents organized so you can respond quickly if an issue arises.
- Review your plan's member handbook for specific appeal instructions and phone numbers.
- Reach out to a trusted advisor if you receive a denial letter or have concerns about coverage.

You deserve for your Medicare coverage to work for you, and these rights ensure you can stand up for the care you need.

In the next chapter, we'll cover Medicare fraud and how to avoid scams, so you can spot danger early and keep your personal information and Medicare benefits safe.

Medicare gives you rights. This chapter gives you the confidence to use them.

Chapter 17

Avoiding Scams and Medicare Fraud

Medicare is one of the most valuable benefits you will ever have, but its importance also makes it a prime target for scammers and fraudsters. Every year, criminals try to steal personal information, enroll people in fake plans, or bill Medicare for services that were never provided. The good news is that you can protect yourself and your benefits by learning to spot the red flags and taking simple, consistent precautions.

In this chapter, we will cover the most common Medicare scams seen in 2026, the clear warning signs to watch for, practical protection strategies you can use right away, and exactly how to report suspicious activity. Staying informed is your strongest defense.

Why Medicare Scams Are So Common

Scammers know that millions of Americans rely on Medicare for their healthcare. They use high-pressure tactics, spoofed phone numbers, fake emails, and even door-to-door visits to trick people into giving up their Medicare numbers, bank details, or personal information. Once they have your Medicare number, they can file fraudulent claims, enroll you in unwanted plans, or steal your identity. Fortunately, most scams follow predictable patterns, and recognizing them early can keep you safe.

Common Medicare Scams in 2026

Here are the schemes that surface most often:

- **Fake "New Medicare Card" Scams:** Callers claim Medicare is issuing a new plastic or chip-enabled card and ask you to "verify" or "activate" it by providing your Medicare number or bank information.

- **Promises of Free Medical Equipment, Tests, or Supplies:** Offers for free catheters, braces, diabetes supplies, genetic tests, or cancer screenings that your doctor never ordered.

- **Pressure to Switch Plans or Enroll "Today":** Unsolicited calls claiming you are "pre-approved" for a better Medicare Advantage or Part D plan with huge savings, often during enrollment periods.

- **Flex Card or Gift Card Bait-and-Switch:** Scammers promise free grocery or over-the-counter benefit cards if you switch plans or provide your information.
- **Hospice or Home Health Enrollment Tricks:** Fake offers to sign you up for "free" hospice or home care services you do not need.
- **Threats That Your Benefits Will Be Canceled:** Urgent warnings that your coverage will end unless you act immediately or pay a fee.

Red Flags: What Should Make You Pause

Train yourself to recognize these immediate warning signs:

- Unsolicited calls, texts, emails, or visits from someone claiming to be from Medicare, Social Security, or your plan.
- Requests for your Medicare number, Social Security number, bank account, or credit card information over the phone or by email.
- High-pressure tactics that demand you decide "right now" or risk losing benefits.

- Promises that sound too good to be true, such as free items, huge savings, or services with no out-of-pocket cost.
- Threats that your Medicare coverage will be terminated if you do not act.
- Offers for services or equipment your doctor has not ordered.
- Suspicious links or attachments in emails or texts asking you to click or download something.

Rule to Live By: Real Medicare representatives will never call, email, or visit you unexpectedly to ask for personal information or demand immediate action. If someone does, hang up or walk away.

Protection Tips You Can Use Today

Follow these straightforward habits to stay safe:

1. **Guard Your Medicare Number:** Treat it like a credit card number. Only share it with your doctors, trusted healthcare providers, or during calls you initiate yourself.
2. **Never Click on Unsolicited Messages:** Ignore links in emails or texts claiming to be from Medicare. Go directly to Medicare.gov instead.

3. **Verify Before You Act**: If someone claims to represent Medicare or your plan, hang up and call the official number on your plan card or 1-800-MEDICARE.

4. **Review Your Statements Regularly:** Check your Medicare Summary Notice (for Original Medicare) or Explanation of Benefits (for Medicare Advantage and Part D) every month. Look for services or equipment you did not receive and report anything suspicious immediately.

5. **Work with Licensed, Trusted Professionals**: Use independent brokers who represent multiple carriers and never pressure you. Avoid anyone who pushes a single plan or asks for payment to enroll you.

6. **Use Official Sources:** Always compare plans or get information directly from Medicare.gov or by calling 1-800-MEDICARE.

Quick Protection Checklist

- Do I recognize the caller or sender?
- Did I initiate this contact?
- Is anyone asking for my Medicare number or banking details?
- Does the offer sound too good to be true?
- Am I being pressured to decide immediately?

If you answer "yes" to any of these, stop and verify through official channels.

Real Talk from a Medicare Broker

In my years helping beneficiaries nationwide, I have seen good people lose time, money, and peace of mind to these scams. The scammers are professional and sound convincing, but they rely on fear and urgency. The beneficiaries who stay safest are the ones who slow down, verify everything, and reach out to a trusted advisor when something feels off. You do not have to handle suspicious contacts alone.

Next Steps

- Set a reminder to review your Medicare statements each month.
- Save the official contact numbers in your phone: 1-800-MEDICARE and your plan's customer service line.
- Discuss these red flags with family members so they can help watch for scams too.
- If you ever feel unsure about a call, email, or offer, contact Medicare.

You deserve to enjoy your Medicare benefits with confidence and without fear of scams.

In the next chapter, we'll cover the importance of annual reviews, so you can confidently evaluate your coverage each fall and make sure you're always getting the best value and protection for your needs.

Stay alert, stay skeptical, and stay protected!

Chapter 18

Annual Review Made Simple

OCTOBER 2026

S	M	T	W	T	F	S
				1	2	3
4	5	6	7	8	9	10
11	12	13	14	(15)	16	17
18	19	20	21	22	23	24
25	26	27	28	29	30	31

Remember, Medicare coverage is not a "set it and forget it" decision. Your health needs, prescription drugs, doctors, budget, and travel habits can change from one year to the next. That is why taking a few minutes each fall to review your current plan can save you hundreds or even thousands of dollars while ensuring you continue to receive the coverage that best fits your life.

In this chapter, we will walk you through why an annual review matters, the simple, step-by-step process for comparing your options, when and how to make changes, and practical tips to maximize your benefits year after year. With a clear system in place, the Annual Election Period becomes an opportunity rather than an overwhelming task.

Why You Should Review Your Medicare Coverage Every Year

Even if you are happy with your current plan, small shifts can make a substantial difference:

- Your prescription drugs may have changed, moved to a higher tier, or no longer be covered.
- Your doctors or preferred hospitals may have left or joined a network.
- New extra benefits (dental, vision, hearing, gym memberships) may now be available at little or no extra cost.
- Your out-of-pocket costs or premiums may have increased more than expected.
- Your overall health or travel plans may have changed.

Reviewing annually puts you back in the driver's seat and prevents small issues from turning into costly surprises.

When to Do Your Annual Review

The official **Annual Election Period (AEP)** runs from **October 15 to December 7** every year. Changes you make during this window take effect on **January 1** of the following year.

You can also make certain changes during other special enrollment periods if you qualify (for example, if you move, lose coverage, or have a major life event). For most people, however, the AEP is the easiest and most powerful time to shop and switch.

Step-by-Step: How to Conduct a Simple Annual Review

Follow this straightforward process each October:

1. **Gather Your Current Information:** Pull out your current Medicare Summary Notice (or Explanation of Benefits), list of prescriptions, and the names of doctors and specialists you see regularly.

2. **Check What Is Changing:** Review your current plan's "Annual Notice of Change" letter (sent in September or October). Pay close attention to:
   - Premium increases
   - Changes to drug coverage or tier levels
   - Network changes
   - Benefit reductions or new restrictions.

3. **Compare Your Options:** Use the Plan Finder tool on Medicare.gov, or work directly with a broker to compare:
   - Medicare Advantage plans (including those with $0 premiums)

- Medigap policies plus a standalone Part D plan
- How each option covers your doctors, prescriptions, and desired extra benefits

4. **Run the Numbers:** Look beyond monthly premiums. Calculate your estimated total yearly cost (premiums + deductibles + copays + coinsurance) based on the care you actually expect to use.

5. **Make Your Decision and Enroll:** If you decide to switch, do it before December 7 with the new plan's effective date of January 1 of the following year.

Key Questions to Ask During Your Review

- Are all my current doctors still in-network?
- Are my prescriptions still covered or at the lowest cost possible?
- Do I need more (or less) dental, vision, or hearing coverage this year?
- Would a plan with a lower out-of-pocket maximum give me better peace of mind?
- Am I paying more than necessary for the benefits I actually use?

- Does a Medigap plan now make more sense for my situation?

Tips to Maximize Benefits Year After Year

- **Take Advantage of Extra Benefits**: Many Medicare Advantage plans offer gym memberships, over-the-counter allowances, transportation, or meal delivery. Use them since they are already paid for in your premium.
- **Use Preventive Services:** Original Medicare and most plans cover annual wellness visits, screenings, and vaccines at no cost. Schedule them early in the year.
- **Stay on Top of Prior Authorizations:** If your new plan requires them, get approvals before you need care.
- **Keep Good Records:** Save your plan documents and comparison notes so next year's review is even easier.
- **Complete Annual Reviews:** Plans may change yearly, so a review ensures you keep the optimal plan for your budget and health needs.

Real Talk from a Medicare Broker

Many beneficiaries tell me they dread the Annual Election Period because it feels confusing or time-consuming. In reality, once you have a simple system and the right help, the review takes less than an hour and often uncovers meaningful savings or better benefits. The clients who review their Medicare coverage every year consistently report less stress and greater confidence in their coverage.

Next Steps
- Mark your calendar now for mid-October to begin your review.
- Gather your current plan documents and medication list in one easy-to-find folder.
- Schedule a free annual Medicare review with a broker who can show you real side-by-side comparisons.

You deserve Medicare coverage that continues to work for you year after year, not just the plan you picked once upon a time.

In the next chapter, we'll cover real stories, common challenges, and solutions, so you can learn from real experiences and feel even more prepared for your own Medicare journey.

The clients who review their coverage every year consistently report less stress and more confidence. You are already ahead of most people by being here.

Chapter 19

Real Stories from the Front Lines

Reading about rules and options is helpful, but nothing brings Medicare to life like hearing real stories from people who have faced the same decisions and challenges you are facing right now. In this chapter, we share anonymous but true experiences from beneficiaries across the country. Each story highlights a common problem, the choices they considered, and how they ultimately found a solution that worked.

These stories are not just case studies. They are powerful reminders that you are not alone, and that with the right information and support, you can navigate Medicare successfully.

Story 1: The Unexpected

Margaret, 68, had been on a popular $0-premium Medicare Advantage plan for three years and loved the extra dental and vision benefits. Then she received her Annual Notice of Change and saw that her favorite dentist was dropping out of the network and that her blood pressure medication had moved to a higher tier.

What she did: Margaret sat down with her medication list and called her Medicare Broker. They ran the current year and projected next year's costs side by side. She discovered that switching to a different Medicare Advantage plan with a slightly higher premium actually lowered her total estimated out-of-pocket costs by over $1,200 a year and kept her current dentist in-network.

Lesson: Never assume your current plan will still be the best value. A quick annual review can uncover significant savings.

Story 2: The Snowbirds Who Got Caught in a Network Trap

Robert and Linda, both 72, split their time between two states. They chose a Medicare Advantage HMO because it had a low premium and included hearing aids. When Robert needed unexpected knee surgery while away from home, the plan denied coverage because the surgeon was out-of-network.

What they did: After the stressful experience, they switched to Original Medicare plus a Medicare Supplement (Medigap) Plan G during the next enrollment period. The higher monthly premium was more than offset by the freedom to see any Medicare-accepting doctor nationwide and the elimination of surprise bills.

Lesson: If you travel regularly or live a snowbird lifestyle, nationwide flexibility often outweighs lower premiums.

Story 3: The Medication Cost Nightmare

Susan, 65, enrolled in a Medicare Advantage plan with prescription coverage. Six months later, one of her cancer-support medications jumped from a $35 copay to $485 because it moved to a specialty tier. Her total monthly drug costs skyrocketed.

What she did: Susan found a standalone Part D plan that covered her medications at a much lower tier. She disenrolled from her Medicare Advantage plan during the Annual Election Period, returned to Original Medicare, added the new Part D plan, and purchased a Medigap policy during her guaranteed issue period. Her monthly drug costs dropped back below $100.

Lesson: Always check your specific prescriptions on the plan's formulary before you enroll. Drug coverage can change dramatically from year to year.

Story 4: The Late Enrollment Penalty Scare

David turned 65, continued working with employer coverage, and delayed signing up for Medicare. When he finally retired at 68, he assumed he could enroll without penalty. He received a Part B late-enrollment penalty because he missed his initial enrollment window and did not have qualifying group coverage for the entire period.

What he did: David gathered proof of his employer coverage and successfully appealed the penalty. He also learned the importance of coordinating benefits with employer plans and now advises every friend approaching 65 to double-check their timeline and current coverage.

Lesson: Understand your enrollment windows and how employer or retiree coverage interacts with Medicare. Remember, small timing mistakes can be expensive.

Story 5: The Appeal That Actually Worked

James received a denial for an expensive MRI that his doctor said was medically necessary. His Medicare Advantage plan said it was "not covered." Frustrated, he almost gave up.

What he did: James obtained a strong letter of medical necessity from his doctor and submitted it to the first level of appeal. The plan reversed its decision within two weeks and covered the full cost of the MRI.

Lesson: Most appeals are winnable when you provide clear medical documentation and follow the deadlines.

Story 6: Successfully Reducing IRMAA

Paul, 71, was surprised when he received a letter from Social Security stating that his 2026 Part B and Part D premiums would be significantly higher due to IRMAA (Income-Related Monthly Adjustment Amount). Based on his income from two years earlier, he was facing an extra $1,800 per year in surcharges. He felt frustrated because his current income had dropped after retirement.

What he did: By working with his tax advisor, Paul completed a Roth IRA conversion in a lower-income year and adjusted some investment withdrawals.

These steps lowered his modified adjusted gross income (MAGI) enough to bring him below the IRMAA threshold for the following year.
Within a few months, his monthly Part B premium returned to the standard amount, saving him over $1,500 annually.

Lesson: IRMAA is based on income from two years prior, so proactive tax planning and timely appeals can often reduce or eliminate these surcharges.

Real Talk from a Medicare Broker

These stories are common, but they do not have to be your story. The beneficiaries who come out ahead are those who ask questions early, review their coverage every year, and reach out for help rather than trying to figure everything out on their own. Every challenge has a solution — sometimes it just takes the right guidance and a little persistence.

Next Steps
- Reflect on which of these stories feels closest to your own situation.
- Make notes about your doctors, medications, travel plans, and budget concerns.
- Schedule a no-obligation Medicare review so you can avoid the pitfalls others have faced.

You deserve Medicare coverage that supports your life instead of complicating it.

In the next chapter, we'll cover Medicare in retirement, so you can build a long-term strategy that protects your health, your finances, and your peace of mind for years to come.

Your story does not have to look like theirs, but it can end just as well!

Chapter 20

Planning Ahead

Medicare is not just about choosing a plan for next year.
It is about building a smart, long-term strategy that
supports your retirement lifestyle, protects your savings,
and gives you peace of mind for decades to come.
Thinking ahead about how Medicare fits into your overall
retirement picture can save you money and prevent
stressful surprises later.

In this chapter, we will explore how Medicare interacts
with retirement income, budgeting, taxes, and the
significant changes already on the horizon. You will walk
away with practical ways to plan effectively so that
Medicare works for you, not against you.

Medicare and Your Retirement Budget

Retirement spending looks vastly different once healthcare costs enter the picture. According to recent estimates, the average couple retiring at 65 can expect to spend $315,000 or more on healthcare throughout retirement, and that is before any major illnesses.

Key budgeting considerations include:

- **Monthly Premiums**: Factor in your Part B premiums, any IRMAA surcharges, any Medicare Advantage or Medigap premiums, and Part D costs.
- **Out-of-Pocket Expenses:** Even with good coverage, deductibles, copays, and coinsurance add up. Build a realistic buffer in your budget.
- **Long-Term Care:** Medicare does not cover custodial long-term care (help with daily activities). Plan separately with long-term care insurance, hybrid life insurance policies, or dedicated savings.
- **Inflation Adjustments:** Healthcare costs typically rise faster than general inflation. Review and increase your healthcare budget accordingly.

A simple approach many retirees use is to set up a dedicated "Healthcare Bucket" in their retirement accounts and automatically transfer money into it each month.

How Medicare Affects Your Taxes

Medicare and taxes are closely connected to retirement:

- **IRMAA Surcharges:** If your modified adjusted gross income (MAGI) from two years prior is above certain thresholds, you will pay higher Part B and Part D premiums. In 2026, these Income-Related Monthly Adjustment Amounts can add hundreds of dollars per month.
- **Roth Conversions:** Strategic Roth IRA conversions in your 60s can help lower future MAGI and reduce or eliminate IRMAA surcharges later.
- **Social Security Taxation:** Up to 85% of your Social Security benefits may be taxable depending on your total income, including Medicare premiums.

- **Health Savings Accounts (HSAs):** If you were eligible for an HSA before enrolling in Medicare, you can continue using tax-free dollars for qualified medical expenses even after you are on Medicare.

Working with a tax advisor who understands Medicare can help you minimize these costs legally and effectively.

What's Changing in Medicare and How to Prepare

Medicare is not static. Here are the major shifts already scheduled or under discussion for the coming years:

- **Rising Part B Premiums and Deductibles**: Expect steady increases as healthcare costs grow.
- **Medicare Advantage Payment Changes:** The government is adjusting how Medicare Advantage plans are paid, which may lead to higher premiums or fewer extra benefits in some plans by 2027–2028.
- **Prescription Drug Reforms**: The Inflation Reduction Act is continuing to take effect, and the cap adjusts annually.
- **Telehealth and Remote Monitoring Expansion**: More services are likely to remain covered long-term, which is especially helpful for rural or mobility-limited beneficiaries.
- **Potential Future Funding Adjustments:** As the baby boomer generation ages, Congress will continue debating ways to keep Medicare solvent, which may affect benefits or eligibility rules down the road.

The best way to stay ahead is to review your plan every year and remain flexible as rules evolve.

Building Your Long-Term Medicare Strategy

Here are practical steps to plan effectively:

1. **Project Your Healthcare Costs**: Estimate your total annual Medicare-related expenses for the next 5–10 years.
2. **Coordinate with Other Income Sources:** Decide when to start Social Security, when to draw from retirement accounts, and how that affects your Medicare premiums.
3. **Consider Medigap vs. Medicare Advantage:** Evaluate which path gives you more predictability as you age and potentially need more care.
4. **Plan for a Spouse or Partner:** Make sure both of your coverages align so one person's change does not create gaps for the other.
5. **Prepare for Long-Term Care:** Medicare stops at skilled care. Build a separate plan for custodial care needs.

Real Talk from a Medicare Broker

I have sat with many retirees who wished they had thought about these bigger-picture issues earlier. The clients who plan ahead sleep better at night because they know their healthcare costs are budgeted, their taxes are optimized, and they are ready for whatever changes come next. It is never too early or too late to start.

Next Steps

- Meet with a financial advisor who understands Medicare to run long-term projections.
- Add healthcare costs to your annual retirement budget review.
- Keep an eye on official Medicare announcements each fall for the latest updates.
- Schedule a comprehensive Medicare and retirement review to align your coverage with your overall financial plan.

You deserve a retirement in which healthcare supports your dreams rather than limiting them.

In the next chapter, we'll cover additional protection options, so you are aware of the other products that may make sense for you and your family. It will arm you with the knowledge to make completely informed decisions.

The best time to plan was yesterday. The second-best time is right now!

Chapter 21

Additional Protection Options

Medicare forms the foundation of your healthcare coverage in retirement, but it is not designed to cover every possible expense. Many people choose to explore supplemental products that can address specific gaps or provide extra financial support during challenging times. These are not required and not right for everyone, but being aware of them helps you make more informed decisions.

In this chapter, we'll briefly introduce some of the most common additional products people consider when enrolling in or reviewing Medicare. The goal is to give you a clear overview so you can decide what, if anything, makes sense for your own situation.

Hospital Indemnity Insurance

Hospital Indemnity (sometimes called Hospital Confinement or Hospital Cash) pays a fixed daily cash benefit when you are admitted to the hospital. You can use this money however you wish. You can use it to help with the Part A deductible and copays, travel costs for family, lost wages for a caregiver, or any other expenses.

It is especially popular with people on Medicare Advantage plans (which often have per-day hospital copays) or those who want a low-cost way to add a financial cushion during an inpatient stay. Benefits are usually straightforward and paid directly to you.

Critical Illness / Cancer, Heart Attack & Stroke Riders (CHAS)

These policies provide a lump-sum cash payment if you are diagnosed with a covered critical illness. The money can help cover:
- Travel for specialized treatment
- Home modifications
- Childcare or caregiver support
- Every day bills while you focus on recovery.

Some plans offer riders for additional conditions or treatments, such as chemotherapy or radiation. These are not health insurance. They are cash benefits intended to ease the financial burden that can accompany a serious diagnosis.

Short-Term Care Insurance

Short-term care policies typically help cover temporary assistance with daily activities (such as bathing, dressing, or eating) for a limited time, often up to 12 months. This can be useful after a hospital stay, surgery, or illness when you need extra help at home or in a short-term facility but do not yet qualify for long-term care insurance benefits.

Medicare covers only short-term skilled nursing or rehabilitation under specific conditions. Short-term care insurance can help fill some gaps in custodial-type support.

Other Optional Products Some People Consider

- **Accident Insurance:** Helps with unexpected injuries from falls or other accidents.
- **Dental, Vision, and Hearing Plans:** Especially useful if your Medicare Advantage plan has limited benefits in these areas.

- **Final Expense / Burial Insurance:** Small whole-life policies designed to help with funeral and burial costs.

These products are all optional and work alongside your Medicare coverage. Premiums are usually modest, but it is important to understand exactly what each policy pays, any exclusions, and how it coordinates with Medicare.

A Few Things to Keep in Mind

- These policies are not substitutes for Medicare, a Medicare Supplement (Medigap), or a solid Medicare Advantage plan.
- Always compare the actual benefits, waiting periods, and costs before deciding.
- Some people find value in one or two of these products; others prefer to build a larger emergency fund instead.
- The right combination (if any) depends on your health, budget, family situation, and peace of mind preferences.

Next Steps

- Add these options to your list of things to discuss during your annual Medicare review.
- Ask questions about how any additional product would work with your current Medicare setup.

- Work only with a licensed, independent advisor who can show you clear, side-by-side information without pressure.

In the next chapter, we'll bring everything together so you can take clear, confident next steps.

Coverage gaps don't announce themselves until it's too late. You've just closed several you didn't even know were open.

Chapter 22

Your Medicare Action Plan

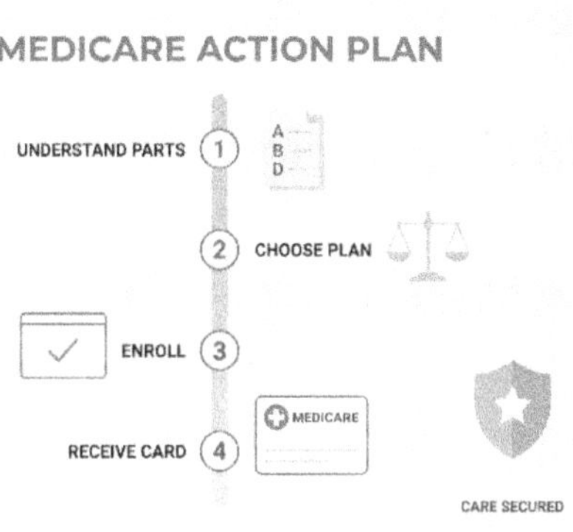

You have now explored the essentials of Medicare: from Parts A and B, prescription drug coverage, Medigap, and Medicare Advantage plans to enrollment, costs, rights, special situations, and how to compare options. Medicare can feel complex at first, but you are now far better equipped to make informed decisions that protect both your health and your finances.

The journey doesn't end here. Medicare evolves every year, and your own needs may change with shifts in health, location, budget, or life events. The key to long-term success is knowing exactly where to turn for reliable, up-to-date, and unbiased help when you need it.

In this chapter, we provide practical checklists, worksheets you can use right away, and the best resources to keep you on track.

Your Medicare Action Plan

Use this simple plan to move forward with confidence:

Immediate Actions (This Week)
- Create or log into your secure Medicare.gov account.
- Make a list of your current doctors and specialists.
- Make a list of your current prescription medications.
- Mark your calendar for your Initial Enrollment Period (IEP) or your Annual Election Period (AEP).

This Month
- Use Medicare.gov/plan-compare to run a personalized comparison using your ZIP code, medications, and preferred doctors.
- Contact your local State Health Insurance Assistance Program (SHIP) for free, unbiased counseling if you have questions.

Ongoing Habits

- Review your healthcare statements every month for accuracy.
- Review your quarterly Medicare Summary Notice (MSN)/Explanation of Benefits (EOB).
- Review your current plan's Annual Notice of Change when received.
- Mark your calendar for the next Annual Election Period (October 15 to December 7)
- Update your medication and doctor list whenever changes occur.
- Revisit your overall retirement budget to ensure healthcare costs are properly accounted for.
- Schedule your yearly Annual Election Period review with your trusted independent Medicare broker.

Helpful Worksheets You Can Use

Doctor & Provider Worksheet: List every doctor and facility you use regularly, along with whether they accept Medicare and are in-network for any Medicare Advantage plans you are considering.

Prescription Medication Worksheet: Write down each medication, dosage, daily quantity, current monthly cost, and which plans cover it at the lowest cost.

Cost Comparison Worksheet: Track monthly premiums, deductibles, estimated copays/coinsurance, and total projected yearly costs for each plan option you are evaluating.

Life Event Tracker: Note any upcoming changes, such as retirement, marriage, divorce, moving, or loss of employer coverage, so that you can act during the correct special enrollment period.

You can create these worksheets on paper or in a simple spreadsheet. Keeping them updated will make every future review much easier.

Official Medicare Resources

Begin with these government-backed tools for the most accurate and current information:

- **Medicare.gov**: The official website for everything Medicare-related. Create or log into your secure Medicare account to view claims, manage prescriptions, switch to electronic notices, and access personalized tools. Use the Plan Finder at Medicare.gov/plan-compare. Enter your ZIP code, medications, and preferred doctors for customized results. You can also check coverage details, find providers through Care Compare, explore preventive services, and download the latest "Medicare & You"

handbook (updated annually). Visit often for updates and helpful new features.

- **1-800-MEDICARE (1-800-633-4227)**: Call for help with enrollment, coverage questions, claims, appeals, or complaints. TTY users dial 1-877-486-2048. Available 24/7 in English and many other languages.

These resources are always free, unbiased, and provided directly by the Centers for Medicare & Medicaid Services (CMS).

Free, Personalized Counseling: State Health Insurance Assistance Programs (SHIP)

For in-depth, one-on-one help without any sales pressure, contact your local State Health Insurance Assistance Program (SHIP). This is a federally funded network of trained counselors available in every state.

SHIP counselors provide objective assistance with enrollment and plan comparisons, understanding costs, appeals, prescription drug coverage, coordinating Medicare with other insurance, and reporting fraud or billing issues.

Services are completely free, local, and independent —
with no ties to insurance companies. To find your SHIP:

- Visit shiphelp.org to locate your state program.
- Call the national SHIP Technical Assistance Center
  at 1-877-839-2675

Additional Helpful Resources

- **Senior Medicare Patrol (SMP)**: Helps detect,
  prevent, and report Medicare fraud, errors, or
  abuse. Find your local program at shiphelp.org or
  call 1-877-808-2468.
- **Extra Help for Prescription Costs**: If your
  income qualifies, this low-income subsidy can
  dramatically reduce or eliminate Part D premiums
  and copays. Check eligibility at Medicare.gov or
  through your SHIP.

Personalized Help from a Trusted Medicare Broker

While official resources and SHIPs provide excellent
general guidance, many people benefit from working
directly with an independent Medicare broker who can
compare dozens of plans side-by-side based on your
specific doctors, medications, budget, and preferences,

handle enrollment paperwork, and provide ongoing annual reviews.

Next Steps: Take Action Today

1. Log in to or create your Medicare.gov account to access personalized tools and your claims history.
2. Use Medicare.gov/plan-compare to preview your options based on your ZIP code, medications, and doctors.
3. Contact your local SHIP for free, unbiased counseling if you have questions.
4. Mark your calendar now for the next Annual Election Period (October 15 to December 7) so you're ready to make any needed changes.

You are more prepared than you realize! You now have everything you need to take confident action. Small steps today will lead to stronger protection tomorrow. You came to this book looking for answers. You are leaving it with a plan.

In the next and final chapter, we will bring everything together with clear closing thoughts to help you move forward with confidence.

Chapter 23

Summary: Your Clear Path Forward With Medicare

Congratulations. You have now completed **Medicare Mastered: A Strategic Guide to Coverage, Costs, and Choices**.

You began this journey with questions and uncertainty. You now understand the foundation of Medicare. You understand Parts A and B, prescription drug coverage through Part D, and the differences between Medicare Advantage and Medigap plans. You discovered how costs really work, enrollment timelines, your rights and appeals process, how to avoid scams, and how to review and adjust your coverage year after year.

Most importantly, you have learned that Medicare is not a one-time decision but an ongoing strategy that should support your health, your budget, and your lifestyle.

Medicare can feel overwhelming at first, but with the right knowledge and support, it becomes manageable and even empowering. You no longer have to fear surprise bills, confusing paperwork, or making the wrong choice. You now have the tools and confidence to take control.

What You Have Learned

Throughout this book, you discovered:

- How Original Medicare works and when it makes sense to add a Medigap policy for predictability and nationwide freedom.
- How Medicare Advantage plans can offer lower premiums and extra benefits, but with network limitations you must understand.
- The importance of reviewing your specific doctors, medications, and budget every year during the Annual Election Period.
- How to protect yourself from common scams and fraud while guarding your personal information.
- Your rights as a beneficiary and exactly how to appeal a denial if something goes wrong.
- How Medicare fits into your broader retirement picture, including budgeting, taxes, and long-term care planning.

You now know that there is no single "best" plan for everyone, only the best plan for **you** at this stage of life.

The Most Important Truth

The beneficiaries who do best with Medicare are not necessarily the ones who pick the perfect plan on day one. They are the ones who stay proactive, review their coverage annually, ask questions when something changes, and reach out for help rather than struggle alone. You have that power now.

Your Final Action Steps

1. **Take one small step this week**: Log into Medicare.gov, update your medication list, or schedule a free Medicare review.
2. **Mark your calendar:** Put your Initial Annual Enrollment Period or the next Annual Election Period on your schedule so you never miss it.
3. **Build your support team:** Know who you will call when questions arise: your SHIP counselor, 1-800-MEDICARE, and an independent broker.
4. **Stay curious:** Medicare changes every year. Continue learning and adjusting as your needs evolve.

Chapter 24

A Final Word

At Care For Healthcare, we believe Medicare should be clear, simple, and worry-free. Jamie Kranking, the owner and a trusted independent Medicare broker, founded Care For Healthcare with one goal in mind: to help people like you understand your options and choose coverage that truly fits your life, without pressure or confusion.

Whether you are just turning 65, already on Medicare, reviewing your options for next year, or helping a loved one, Jamie and the team are always happy to offer honest, no-obligation guidance. They can sit down with you (by phone, video, or in person), run personalized plan comparisons, and answer any questions you still have.

You are welcome to reach out anytime. Visit **www.careforhealthcare.com** or email jamie@careforhealthcare.com.   This is NEVER a sales pitch. We provide clear answers and friendly support.

Thank you for reading **Medicare Mastered**. My sincere hope is that this book has removed much of the confusion and given you the confidence to navigate Medicare successfully for many years to come.

Glossary

Annual Election Period

The period that runs from October 15 to December 7 each year. During this period, Medicare beneficiaries can enroll in, change, or disenroll from a Medicare Advantage Plan or a Part D prescription drug plan.

Annual Notice of Change (ANOC)

The Annual Notice of Change (ANOC) is an official document that Medicare Advantage plans (Part C) and Medicare Part D prescription drug plans must send to all current enrollees every year, typically in September or early October.

Beneficiary

A person who receives their health care coverage through Medicare.

Benefit Period

A Medicare Part A benefit period is the way Original Medicare measures and pays for your inpatient hospital care and skilled nursing facility services. It begins the day you are formally admitted as an inpatient to a hospital or skilled nursing facility. The benefit period ends only after you have been out of the hospital or skilled nursing facility for 60 consecutive days. You may have several benefit periods in a single calendar year, and each new benefit period starts your Part A deductible again and gives you a fresh set of 90 inpatient hospital days plus up to 100 skilled nursing facility days. Understanding benefit periods is important because a readmission within 60 days continues the same benefit period and does not reset your deductible or day counts.

Catastrophic Coverage Limit

The Catastrophic Coverage Limit is the final stage of the Medicare Part D prescription drug benefit, where you pay very little out-of-pocket for covered medications for the rest of the calendar year.

COBRA (Consolidated Omnibus Budget Reconciliation Act)

COBRA is a federal law that lets you keep your employer-sponsored group health insurance after you leave your job, reduce your hours, or experience certain qualifying events. You can usually continue the exact same coverage for up to 18 months (sometimes longer) by paying the full premium yourself plus a small administrative fee.

Coinsurance

The percentage of the Medicare-approved amount you pay after the deductible (usually 20% for Part A and B services).

Community Rating

Community Rating is a pricing rule used by Medigap insurance companies in most states that requires insurers to charge the same monthly premium to everyone who buys the same Medicare

Supplement Plans (Medigap) plan in the same area, regardless of age, gender, or health status. Once you are accepted during your Medicare Open Enrollment period, the insurance company cannot charge you more or deny coverage based on pre-existing conditions. This protection makes Medigap rates fairer and more predictable for retirees compared to states that allow medical underwriting and attained-age rating.

Copay

A fixed dollar amount you pay for a specific service or drug after you meet your deductible.

Creditable Coverage

Creditable coverage is Medicare's way of saying that another health insurance plan provides adequate health and prescription coverage that is at least as good as Original Medicare Part A and B, as well as Prescription coverage Medicare Part D.

Deductible

The amount you must pay out-of-pocket before Medicare or your plan begins to pay benefits.

Drug Tier

Medications on a Part D drug formulary are grouped into tiers that determine your portion of the drug cost. Generic medications would be considered at a lower, more cost-effective tier.

Durable Medical Equipment

Medical equipment that is ordered or prescribed by a doctor, such as canes, crutches, hospital beds, oxygen equipment, walkers, and wheelchairs.

End-Stage Renal Disease (ESRD)

End Stage Renal Disease (ESRD) is a permanent form of kidney failure in which the kidneys can no longer function well enough to keep you alive without dialysis or a kidney transplant. Medicare has special eligibility rules for people with ESRD, allowing them to qualify for coverage regardless of age.

Formulary

The list of prescription drugs covered by your Part D or Medicare Advantage plan is organized into tiers with different costs.

Guaranteed Renewable

Guaranteed Renewable means your insurance company cannot cancel your coverage because of changes in your health. A Medigap plan is a good example. Once you're enrolled, the carrier can only cancel your policy if you stop paying your premium.

General Enrollment Period (GEP)

The General Enrollment Period is the annual window from January 1 through March 31. This is for anyone who missed their Initial

Enrollment Period or wants to make certain Medicare changes, and can sign up for Medicare Part A and/or Part B.

Guaranteed-Issue

Guaranteed Issue is a Medicare rule that requires Medigap insurance companies to sell you a policy and cannot deny coverage or charge you more based on your health, age, or pre-existing conditions. You qualify for Guaranteed Issue rights during specific protected periods, such as when you first become eligible for Medicare, when you lose certain other coverage, or during a trial right period with a Medicare Advantage plan. During these windows, insurers must accept you and offer at least one standardized Medicare Supplement Plan (Medigap) at their community-rated or issue-age-rated premium.

Health Maintenance Organization (HMO)

An HMO (Health Maintenance Organization) is a type of Medicare Advantage (Part C) plan that requires you to use a network of doctors, hospitals, and other providers for all covered services, except in emergencies. You must choose a primary care physician (PCP) who coordinates your care, and you generally need a referral from that PCP to see specialists. If you go outside the network, the plan usually pays nothing, leaving you responsible for the full cost.

Home Health Care

Home Health Care is a Medicare-covered benefit that provides skilled medical services in your own home when you are homebound and need intermittent care. It includes services such as skilled nursing, physical therapy, occupational therapy, speech therapy, and medical social services ordered by your doctor. Medicare does not cover long-term custodial care, such as bathing, dressing, or housekeeping. It only covers short-term skilled care that is medically necessary. Certain conditions must be met to qualify for most home health care.

Hospice Care

Hospice Care is a special Medicare benefit that provides comfort-focused medical care, pain relief, and emotional support for people with a terminal illness who have a life expectancy of six months or less if the illness runs its normal course. Instead of seeking curative treatment, the patient elects hospice and receives services such as nursing care, doctor visits, medications for symptom control, medical equipment, supplies, and bereavement support for the family. Medicare covers hospice care under Part A when a doctor certifies the terminal prognosis.

Initial Enrollment Period

The Initial Enrollment Period is the seven-month window around your 65th birthday when you can first enroll in Medicare without late penalties. It begins three months before the month you turn 65, includes your birthday month, and ends three months after. If your birthday falls on the first of the month, the period starts 4 months before your birthday month and ends 2 months after. For most people, the best time to enroll is during the three months before your birthday month, so your Medicare coverage can start on the first day of your birthday month. During the IEP, you can sign up for Part A and Part B. You can also sign up for Part C with a Prescription Plan included or sign up for a Medigap Plan and a standalone Part D prescription plan.

IRMAA (Income-Related Monthly Adjustment Amount)

The Income-Related Monthly Adjustment Amount is an extra surcharge added to Part B and/or Part D for higher-income beneficiaries based on your tax return from two years earlier.

Late Enrollment Penalty

The Late Enrollment Penalty is a permanent increase added to your monthly Medicare Part B and/or Part D premium if you do not enroll when you first become eligible and do not have other creditable coverage. For Part B, the penalty is usually 10% of the monthly premium for each full 12-month period you delayed enrollment, and it lasts for as long as you have Medicare. For Part D, the penalty is 1% of the national base beneficiary premium for every month you delay, and it is also lifelong. These penalties are added to your premium every month for the rest of your life unless you qualify for a Special Enrollment Period.

Low-Income Subsidy

This is a federal program that helps reduce Part D medication costs for certain low-income Medicare beneficiaries.

Maximum Out-of-Pocket (MOOP)

The Maximum Out-of-Pocket (MOOP) is the most you will have to pay in a calendar year for covered medical services under a

Medicare Advantage plan before the plan pays 100% of the approved amount for the rest of the year. Once you reach your plan's MOOP, you pay nothing more for in-network covered services for the remainder of the year. This does not include Part D drugs. The MOOP does not apply to Original Medicare or Medicare Supplement Plans (Medigap) policies.

Medicare Advantage Open Enrollment Period (MA-OEP)

The MA-OEP runs from January 1 to March 31 each year. If you are already enrolled in a Medicare Advantage plan, you can make one change during this period: switch to a different Medicare Advantage plan or return to Original Medicare (and add a Part D plan if needed). Changes usually start the first day of the following month.

Medicare Summary Notice (MSN) / Explanation of Benefits (EOB)

The MSN is the quarterly explanation of benefits statement that Medicare provides to show services received and what Medicare paid toward them. You should review your MSN to determine if you have any balances due.

Medigap

A Medigap policy is a private health insurance plan sold by insurance companies that helps pay the out-of-pocket costs that Original Medicare (Part A and Part B) does not cover, such as deductibles, coinsurance, and copayments. There are ten standardized Medicare Supplement Plans (Medigap) plans labeled A through N, and each plan offers the same basic benefits regardless of which company sells it. Medicare Supplement Plans (Medigap) work only with Original Medicare and cannot be used with a Medicare Advantage plan.

Open Enrollment Period

The Open Enrollment Period, also known as the Annual Election Period, is the annual window from October 15 to December 7 when anyone with Medicare can make changes to their coverage for the following year.

Original Medicare

Original Medicare is the traditional fee-for-service Medicare program run directly by the federal government. It consists of Part A (hospital insurance) and Part B (medical insurance). Under Original Medicare, you can visit any doctor, hospital, or provider in the United States that accepts Medicare, and the government pays its share of the approved amount for covered services. Original Medicare does not include prescription drug coverage, so most people add a separate Part D plan and/or a Medigap policy to help cover deductibles, coinsurance, and copayments.

Primary Payer

The primary payer is the insurance plan that pays first on a medical claim and covers its share of the approved amount according to its own rules. When you have Medicare and other coverage, the primary payer is responsible for processing the bill before any secondary insurance steps in.

Secondary Payer

The secondary payer is the insurance plan that pays after the primary payer has paid its portion. It covers some or all of the remaining costs not covered by the primary payer. Medigap policies act as a secondary payer to Original Medicare by helping pay deductibles, coinsurance, and copayments that Original Medicare leaves behind.

SHIP (State Health Insurance Assistance Program)

The federal State Health Insurance Assistance Program is free, with unbiased Medicare counseling available in every state.

Special Enrollment Period (SEP)

A Special Enrollment Period (SEP) is a designated window outside the standard Initial or Annual Enrollment Periods that allows you to enroll in, switch, or disenroll from Medicare plans without penalty. SEPs are triggered by qualifying life events, such as losing employer coverage or moving. The length of the SEP and available changes depend on the specific event.

Trial Right SEP

A Medicare Advantage Trial Right SEP is a one-time protection. This protection is a 12-month period that allows beneficiaries to test a Medicare Advantage plan and switch back to Original Medicare, with guaranteed issue rights to buy a Medigap policy if they are dissatisfied.

TRICARE For Life (TFL)

Health insurance coverage that pays secondary to Medicare for eligible retired service members and their families. TFL functions as a supplemental coverage to Medicare. TFL covers prescription drugs through the TRICARE Pharmacy program.

This glossary is a quick reference. Refer back to it anytime you encounter unfamiliar terms.

About the Author

Jamie Kranking is the founder and owner of **Care For Healthcare**, a Medicare-focused insurance agency dedicated to helping seniors and their families navigate the often-confusing world of Medicare with clarity, confidence, and care. Residing in Florida, Jamie helps clients nationally. He has guided thousands of clients through Medicare decisions, ensuring they select the right coverage for their health needs, budget, and lifestyle without costly mistakes.

Jamie did not begin his career in insurance. For many years, he thrived as a high-tech executive at a large software company. Everything changed when his wife, Renee, was diagnosed with Stage IV breast cancer. Suddenly, the couple faced the realities of life outside employer group coverage. Renee transitioned to SSDI and qualified for Medicare, and Jamie dove deeply into researching every option to secure the best possible protection for her.

That personal journey became a powerful turning point. Jamie realized how many families, especially those dealing with serious illness, disability, or retirement transitions, struggle with Medicare decisions alone. He left the corporate world behind to pursue a more meaningful mission: simplifying Medicare for others so they never have to face uncertainty or unnecessary financial stress.

Today, through **Care For Healthcare** (www.careforhealthcare.com), Jamie provides free, unbiased guidance on Medicare, Medicare Advantage, Medicare Supplements (Medigap), Part D prescription plans, and more. He is passionate about education and about breaking down complex rules into clear, actionable steps. It is important to him to stand beside clients year after year as their trusted advocate.

Helping people protect their health and retirement savings has become Jamie's most rewarding work. His personal experience fuels every conversation, online seminar, and chapter, because he knows firsthand how the right Medicare choices can bring peace of mind during life's most challenging chapters.

You can reach Jamie at jamie@careforhealthcare.com.

Resources

Medicare.gov

The official website for plan comparison, claims history, preventive services, and the "Medicare & You" handbook.

1-800-MEDICARE (1-800-633-4227) – 24/7 help with enrollment, appeals, and questions (TTY: 1-877-486-2048).

Free, Unbiased Counseling

State Health Insurance Assistance Programs (SHIP) – Free, local, one-on-one Medicare counseling. Visit shiphelp.org to find your state program or call 1-877-839-2675.

Fraud & Abuse Reporting

Senior Medicare Patrol: 1-877-808-2468

Care For Healthcare

Jamie Kranking and the team at Care For Healthcare offer free, no-obligation Medicare guidance and plan comparisons. Visit www.careforhealthcare.com whenever you would like friendly, unbiased support.

Sources

The information in this book is based on official U.S. government publications, Centers for Medicare & Medicaid Services (CMS) announcements, and Social Security Administration resources. All figures, rules, and deadlines reflect the most current data available for the 2026 plan year. Medicare policies, premiums, deductibles, and benefits change annually, so readers should always verify the latest information directly from official sources such as Medicare.gov or 1-800-MEDICARE.

Key Official Sources

Centers for Medicare & Medicaid Services (CMS). *Medicare & You 2026*. Baltimore, MD: U.S. Department of Health and Human Services; 2025. Available at: https://www.medicare.gov/publications/10050-medicare-and-you.pdf

Centers for Medicare & Medicaid Services. 2026 Medicare Parts A & B Premiums and Deductibles. CMS Fact Sheet. November 2025. Available at: https://www.cms.gov/newsroom/fact-sheets/2026-medicare-parts-b-premiums-deductibles

Centers for Medicare & Medicaid Services. 2026 Medicare Advantage and Part D Rate Announcement and Final Call Letter. April 2025. Available at: https://www.cms.gov/medicare/payment/medicare-advantage-rates-statistics

Centers for Medicare & Medicaid Services. 2026 Medicare Prescription Drug Coverage (Part D) Out-of-Pocket Cap and Deductible Limits. CMS Announcement. November 2025. Available at: https://www.cms.gov/medicare/part-d-prescription-drug-coverage

Centers for Medicare & Medicaid Services. Medicare Supplement Insurance (Medigap) Policies: Standardized Plans Chart. Updated 2026. Available at: https://www.medicare.gov/supplements-other-insurance/how-to-compare-medigap-policies

Centers for Medicare & Medicaid Services. Medicare Advantage and Part D Enrollment Periods. 2026 Guide. Available at: https://www.medicare.gov/basics/get-started-with-medicare/sign-up/enrollment-periods

Centers for Medicare & Medicaid Services. Coordination of Benefits: Medicare and Other Insurance. 2026. Available at: https://www.medicare.gov/what-medicare-covers/coordination-of-benefits

Centers for Medicare & Medicaid Services. Medicare Appeals Process. 2026 Overview. Available at: https://www.medicare.gov/claims-appeals

Centers for Medicare & Medicaid Services. State Health Insurance Assistance Programs (SHIPs). 2026 Directory. Available at: https://shiphelp.org

Centers for Medicare & Medicaid Services. Medicare Fraud & Abuse: Report Suspected Fraud. 2026. Available at: https://www.medicare.gov/basics/reporting-medicare-fraud-and-abuse

Centers for Medicare & Medicaid Services. Extra Help with Prescription Drug Costs. 2026 Eligibility and Application Guide. Available at: https://www.medicare.gov/drug-coverage-part-d/costs/extra-help

Social Security Administration. Your Social Security Statement and IRMAA Information. 2026. Available at: https://www.ssa.gov/myaccount

These sources were consulted to ensure accuracy as of the publication of this edition. For the most current information or personalized questions about any rule or cost in this book, visit Medicare.gov, call 1-800-MEDICARE (1-800-633-4227), or contact your local State Health Insurance Assistance Program (SHIP).

9 798995 489801